BRANCH LINE BRITAIN
LOCAL PASSENGER TRAINS IN THE DIESEL ERA

Front upper: 26021 waits to depart from Georgemas Junction with the Thurso portion of the afternoon train from Inverness on 14 August 1981. *(Paul Shannon)*

Front lower: Single car 55021 calls at Castle Bar Park with the 1236 from Greenford to London Paddington on 31 October 1988. *(Paul Shannon)*

Front flap: Class 101 cars E50162, E59100 and E50200 arrive at Glaisdale with a train from Whitby on 19 July 1982. *(Paul Shannon)*

Rear: Cars M56336 and M51193 wait between duties at Barmouth on 21 September 1978. *(Paul Shannon)*

Rear flap: M51179 and M56358 pull away from Gobowen with a train for Chester on 11 August 1982. *(Paul Shannon)*

BRANCH LINE BRITAIN

LOCAL PASSENGER TRAINS IN THE DIESEL ERA

Paul D. Shannon

PEN & SWORD
TRANSPORT

AN IMPRINT OF PEN & SWORD BOOKS LTD.
YORKSHIRE – PHILADELPHIA

First published in Great Britain in 2023 by
Pen and Sword Transport
An imprint of
Pen & Sword Books Ltd.
Yorkshire - Philadelphia

Copyright © Paul D. Shannon, 2023

ISBN 978 1 39908 990 6

The right of Paul D. Shannon to be identified as author of this work has been asserted by him in accordance with the Copyright, Designs and Patents Act 1988.

A CIP catalogue record for this book is
available from the British Library.

All rights reserved. No part of this book may be reproduced or transmitted in any form or by any means, electronic or mechanical including photocopying, recording or by any information storage and retrieval system, without permission from the Publisher in writing.

Typeset by SJmagic DESIGN SERVICES, India.
Printed and bound by Printworks Global Ltd, London/Hong Kong.

Pen & Sword Books Ltd incorporates the imprints of Pen & Sword Books Archaeology, Atlas, Aviation, Battleground, Discovery, Family History, History, Maritime, Military, Naval, Politics, Railways, Select, Transport, True Crime, Fiction, Frontline Books, Leo Cooper, Praetorian Press, Seaforth Publishing, Wharncliffe and White Owl.

For a complete list of Pen & Sword titles please contact
PEN & SWORD BOOKS LIMITED
George House, Units 12 & 13, Beevor Street, Off Pontefract Road,
Barnsley, South Yorkshire, S71 1HN, England
E-mail: enquiries@pen-and-sword.co.uk
Website: www.pen-and-sword.co.uk

or
PEN AND SWORD BOOKS
1950 Lawrence Rd, Havertown, PA 19083, USA
E-mail: uspen-and-sword@casematepublishers.com
Website: www.penandswordbooks.com

CONTENTS

	Introduction	6
CHAPTER 1	South West England	7
CHAPTER 2	London and the South East	24
CHAPTER 3	East Anglia and Lincolnshire	47
CHAPTER 4	The Midlands	64
CHAPTER 5	Wales	81
CHAPTER 6	North West England	100
CHAPTER 7	Yorkshire and the North East	118
CHAPTER 8	Scotland	136
	Bibliography	152

INTRODUCTION

This book takes a detailed look at how Britain's branch lines and other secondary routes have evolved over the last half century. The starting point is the immediate aftermath of Dr Richard Beeching's infamous 1963 report 'The Reshaping of British Railways', usually referred to simply as the 'Beeching Report' even though its author was not actually named. While that report proposed the closure of some main lines, its main targets were branch lines and other secondary routes where traffic levels were low and operating costs disproportionately high.

Between 1963 and 1970, nearly 4,000 route miles were lost from the British network. Some rural districts were deprived of railways altogether, including parts of Lincolnshire, North Cornwall, parts of Mid-Wales and the Scottish Borders. But some of the remotest parts of the country had their rail connection reprieved, such as the Cumbrian Coast and the Far North of Scotland. Social as well as economic factors were increasingly taken into account when the fate of threatened lines was being determined. After 1970, the closures were few and far between. The high-profile reprieve of the Settle to Carlisle and Kyle of Lochalsh lines heralded a change in policy, as the emphasis switched from wholesale closure to less drastic cost-cutting measures such as track rationalisation and reductions in station staff.

At the same time, BR began to realise the potential to open or reopen small stations as a means of attracting extra business. With Paytrain operation, the running costs of additional stations were relatively low. Local authorities often contributed to the capital expenditure, notably in South and West Yorkshire but also in some more rural areas. The number of stations added to the national network rose from about 50 in the 1970s to more than 100 in the 1980s; these figures included some main-line railheads such as Alfreton & Mansfield Parkway, but most were essentially local facilities. The reopening trend continued into the early 1990s. More than seventy stations joined the national network between 1990 and 1994. They included a good number in Scotland and South Wales, plus the Robin Hood Line in Nottinghamshire.

Electrification projects gathered pace in the 1980s. While many schemes focused on long-distance main lines, a number of branch lines and other secondary routes were wired, such as Wickford-Southminster, Watford Junction-St Albans Abbey and Ardrossan-Largs. Moving into the 1990s, overhead electrification was extended to branches such as North Berwick and Ilkley, while third-rail electrification schemes were completed on the Wirral as well as on the former Southern Region. Electrification often brought an increase in service quality and frequency, even if the trains themselves were not brand new.

As British Rail gave way to the era of private operators, so the rate of station openings and re-openings slowed. This was partly because of the huge cost increase caused by the need to make stations safer, more secure and more accessible. However, the re-openings did not stop altogether. Among the major schemes were the return of passenger trains to two former freight-only lines in South Wales – Barry-Bridgend in 2005 and the Ebbw Vale branch in 2008 – and the revival of the mothballed Stirling-Alloa line in 2008. But by far the most ambitious and ground-breaking scheme was the return of trains to 30 miles of the former Waverley route in 2015, despite parts of the trackbed having been blocked by development. Scotland has also led the way in terms of electrification, with several extensions in and around the Central Belt completed in recent decades.

Not surprisingly, the rolling stock fleet used on local lines has been completely replaced in the last 50 years. The oldest photographs in this book show a wide variety of first-generation DMUs and EMUs, introduced in the 1950s and 1960s to replace costly and cumbersome steam-hauled operations. Sprinters and other types of second-generation unit began to take over in the 1980s and there has also been more than one experiment with low-cost traction, notably the four-wheel Pacers that could still be seen until recently and the Vivarail D-Train that is lurching into service on a few rural routes. But locomotive haulage is represented in these pages as well. Some lines retained their Mark 1 stock for a long time, notably the various branches in the North and North West of Scotland. Some routes elsewhere reverted to locomotive haulage because of a shortage of suitable units, such as Trans-Pennine services in the 1980s and East Anglian branches and the Cumbrian Coast in more recent times.

CHAPTER 1

SOUTH WEST ENGLAND

The physical geography of Cornwall with its long spine and deeply indented coastline lent itself to the building of branch lines. By the early 1960s none of the Cornish branches were carrying more than 5,000 passengers a week and most were proposed for closure in the Beeching Report. Only Falmouth and Newquay were expected to escape the axe. As things turned out, the branches to St Ives and Looe also survived, together with part of the former Callington branch as far as Gunnislake.

The Helston branch was already under threat when the Report was published and it closed to passengers in November 1962. It was a similar story for the meandering Chacewater-Newquay line, which closed in February 1963. The demise of Lostwithiel-Fowey passenger services followed in January 1965, although the single track winding its way alongside the Fowey estuary still carries trainloads of china clay for export today. The former Southern branches to Bude and Padstow via Launceston closed in October 1966 and the remaining route to Padstow via Bodmin succumbed three months later. The Callington branch was cut back to Gunnislake in November 1966. Alongside the various Cornish branch line closures, six intermediate stations on the Plymouth-Penzance main line lost their passenger services in 1964.

Passenger carryings on the St Ives branch increased rapidly after the opening of Lelant Saltings in 1978 and a single carriage was inadequate in the summer months. Arriving in the bay platform at St Erth on 27 July 1983 is a four-car formation comprising Class 121 car W55025 and Class 118 cars W51323, W59475 and W51308. *(Paul Shannon)*

The St Ives branch was effectively reduced to a long siding from St Erth in the 1960s and its terminus was relocated in 1971 to make way for a car park. Class 118 car W51308 is closest to the camera in this view of St Ives dated 27 July 1983. This vehicle and its two partners were no strangers to the South West, having been allocated new to Plymouth Laira in 1960; however they moved between several different Western Region depots from 1962 before returning eventually to their home ground. *(Paul Shannon)*

The combination of Network SouthEast red, white and blue and Great Western style chocolate and cream makes a curious sight as Class 117 cars 51361 and 51368 prepare to depart from St Ives with the 1435 to St Erth on 17 July 1996. Car 51361 had spent most of its life working commuter trains in the Thames Valley but had been reallocated to the South West in 1994. Both vehicles were retired from service in 1997. *(David J. Hayes)*

The 4¼-mile branch from St Erth to St Ives was listed for closure in 1963 but later saved because of its social importance. The route was always single-track and, following the withdrawal of goods facilities, became in effect a long siding from St Erth. The track was shortened by 200 yards in 1971 when the ex-GWR terminus was replaced by a simpler facility to make way for a car park. At that time, BR served St Ives with a shuttle service of thirteen trains each way on weekdays, mostly to and from St Erth but with one through working to and from Penzance. In May 1978 the branch gained an enhanced role with the opening of Lelant Saltings halt, promoted as a 'park and ride' location so that motorists could avoid the congested streets of St Ives. That facility switched to St Erth in 2019, leaving Lelant Saltings with just one call each way on weekdays. However, the branch as a whole still thrives and currently boasts a weekday service of twenty-eight trains each way.

The Falmouth branch lost both its intermediate passing loops in the 1960s and its passenger terminus was relocated to a new site just over 900 yards up the line in 1970. However, the original terminus reopened in 1975; the 1970 platform then became The Dell and, from 1989, Falmouth Town. The service in 1973 comprised just twelve trains each way on weekdays, all running to or from Truro. An improvement came in 2009 when Penryn gained a new passing loop, funded jointly by the European Union, Cornwall County Council and Network Rail. Today's train service amounts to thirty out and back journeys each weekday.

Newquay has always been the most important of the Cornish branch termini. Although it was listed in the Beeching Report, this was for closure of the five

Class 121 car W55033 approaches Truro with a relief working on the Cornish main line on 5 August 1982. The 'Avon Link' sticker provides a clue that this vehicle's home depot was Bristol Bath Road. Centre stage is Truro signal box, dating back to 1899 but with an enlarged frame installed in 1971. Mechanical signalling is still in charge at this location today. *(Paul Shannon)*

intermediate stations rather than wholesale service withdrawal. As it happened, the intermediate stations remained open, but the number of passing loops was reduced to two and the terminus eventually cut back to a single platform. In 1973, Newquay had just six all-stations services to and from Par each weekday, but it also welcomed a number of dated locomotive-hauled holiday trains; there were departures to Sheffield and Liverpool on Fridays and to Manchester, Newcastle, London and Nottingham on Saturdays. Today's timetable has slightly more local trains to and from Par but fewer summer-only long-distance services, the latter taking the place of local trains in the timetable.

The Looe branch must rank as one of the most curious survivors on the British network, the route starting from Liskeard with a sharply curved descent to Coombe where all trains reverse. It was earmarked for closure by Dr Beeching but ultimately retained on grounds of social need. The line was always single-track and there was only ever one platform at Looe, which was relocated about 100 yards up the line in 1968. Coombe Junction lost its signal box in favour of a ground frame in 1981. The train service between Liskeard and Looe has grown from nine trains each way in 1973 to fifteen today, but only two are booked to call at Coombe Junction Halt, as it is now called.

The 9½-mile branch from Bere Alston to Callington, straddling the Devon-Cornwall boundary, was an easy target for Beeching era cuts as its patronage was well below 5,000 passengers a week. However, the section between Bere Alston and Gunnislake was retained because it provided an important link to Plymouth for communities poorly served by road. After Okehampton-Plymouth trains were withdrawn in May 1968, the Bere Alston-Plymouth line was combined with the remaining branch to Gunnislake, with a reversal at Bere Alston.

BR ran nine trains each weekday on the branch in 1973 and its successor 'Great Western Railway' achieves the same total today.

In Devon, the Beeching Report envisaged the closure of all railways except the ex-GWR main line from Taunton to Exeter and Plymouth, the ex-LSWR line from Exeter towards Salisbury, and the branches to Kingswear, Barnstaple and Okehampton. In the event, most but not all of those closures went ahead. Early casualties were the Hemyock branch, Exeter-Dulverton and branches to Kingsbridge and Brixham. They were already under threat before the Report. Several other routes had closed to passengers by the end of the 1960s, the most significant being the former LSWR main line from Okehampton to Tavistock and Bere Alston.

The ex-LSWR branch from Barnstaple to Ilfracombe managed to soldier on until October 1970, although the track had been singled a few years earlier and the passenger service on winter weekdays had shrunk to five trains a day. Next for the chop was Crediton to Okehampton in June 1972. That line had already been singled and the junction with the Barnstaple branch had been moved back to Crediton, with independent single lines between Crediton and Coleford. However, unlike Ilfracombe, the Okehampton branch remained open for freight, mainly ballast from Meldon Quarry. The station at Okehampton also remained intact and this allowed a gradual resumption of passenger services, starting with Devon County Council's 'Dartmoor Rambler' trains on four summer Saturdays in 1984. Okehampton formally re-joined the national network in November 2021, with an initial two-hourly service from Exeter by Great Western Railway increasing to hourly frequency in May 2022.

Carnon Viaduct is arguably the most impressive engineering structure on the 8-mile Falmouth branch. It was completed in 1933 to replace an earlier timber viaduct. Class 118 cars W41325, W59471 and W51310 form the 1630 Falmouth-Truro service on 5 August 1982. At that time the Falmouth branch was single track throughout, although there were still sidings at the Falmouth end for potential freight traffic. *(Paul Shannon)*

St Dennis Junction marked the divergence of the Meledor Mill branch from the Par-Newquay line. It also provided a passing loop for Newquay trains. A Class 118 unit led by car W41325 pauses for the token exchange at St Dennis Junction while working the 1515 service from Par on 2 August 1982. The Meledor Mill branch had then recently been taken out of use, and St Dennis Junction box and loop closed in December 1986. *(Paul Shannon)*

Unlike the other Cornish branch termini, Newquay still had a run-round loop for locomotive-hauled trains in the 1980s. 47447 approaches Middleway crossing near St Blazey with the 0938 Newquay-Plymouth train on 5 August 1982. The lower of the two signal arms gives access to St Blazey yard and would have been used by china clay trains from Pontsmill and Goonbarrow at that time. *(Paul Shannon)*

A Class 119 cross-country unit comprising cars W51072, W59431 and W51085 enters Liskeard station with a Down stopping train on 11 June 1980. The Class 119s spent much of their lives on the Western Region, although in their later years some were based in the Midlands and North East. This particular unit spent only six months in the South West before returning to South Wales. *(Paul Shannon)*

Another non-closure was the 6¾-mile branch extension from Paignton to Kingswear. BR withdrew its passenger service from this route in October 1972, but the Dart Valley Railway moved in straight away and kept the line open – in the summer months at least – as a tourist attraction. An initial all-year-round service for local people lasted only one season. Today, the Dartmouth Steam Railway operates mainly steam-hauled trains between Paignton and Kingswear throughout the summer season and on certain dates in the winter.

While the Paignton-Kingswear line is very much a self-contained operation, now with its own station at Paignton Queens Park, the branch from Newton Abbot to Paignton remains an integral part of the national network, served by a mixture of local and long-distance trains operated by Great Western Railway and CrossCountry.

Heading east from Exeter, the Exmouth branch was a surprise inclusion in the Beeching hit list as it carried more than 50,000 passengers a week. Sure enough, no closure proposal was published and the line remains open today. A new intermediate station at Lympstone Commando opened in 1976, giving access to the adjacent military base, while the remaining single track at Exmouth was shortened by 42 feet in 1975. Two further intermediate stations, Digby & Sowton and Newcourt, opened in 1995 and 2015 respectively. The retention of Topsham loop allows Great Western Railway to run a half-hourly service on the branch, most forming through workings to and from Paignton.

Across Somerset and Dorset, the outlook was bleak in the 1960s for many rural routes. The cross-country lines from Taunton to Chard Junction and Yatton-Wells-Witham were already proposed for closure before the Beeching Report. Among the newly targeted lines was the long, meandering former Somerset and Dorset Joint Railway from Bath Green Park to Bournemouth, which closed in March 1966 along with its offshoot from Evercreech Junction to Highbridge.

The seaside town of Weymouth was home to an unusual, and latterly unique, branch line – the 1¼-mile Weymouth Quay tramway. Main-line passenger trains mingled with road vehicles and pedestrians from the late nineteenth century until regular

In the late 1980s some local trains on the West of England Main Line reverted to locomotive haulage, using short rakes of Mark 1 stock. Carrying the early version of Network SouthEast livery, 50018 *Resolution* crosses Bolitho Viaduct, just east of Liskeard, with the 1525 Penzance-Plymouth working on 17 February 1988. *(Paul Shannon)*

Most Class 118 formations included a centre trailer car, but Laira depot had two twin sets in the early 1970s. One of those sets, comprising cars W51327 and W51312, stands at the branch platform at Liskeard before working the 1755 departure to Looe on 9 September 1973. This platform sits at right angles to the main-line platforms, which are behind the photographer, and is still in use today. *(David Rapson)*

A Class 118 set comprising cars W51313, W59483 and W51316 sets off noisily from the diminutive platform at Coombe Junction with a lunchtime train to Looe on 11 June 1980. The track on the right leads to Moorswater china clay works. Coombe Junction box closed in May 1981 and the layout was simplified with just one track serving the platform and continuing to Moorswater. The signals were removed and the points were then operated by the train guard from a ground frame. *(Paul Shannon)*

The passengers enjoy an uncluttered view of the tidal Looe River as Class 121 single car W55026 heads north from Looe with the 1005 to Liskeard on 2 August 1982. This vehicle spent most of its working life on the Western Region; it had been refurbished and repainted in blue and grey livery in 1981. *(Paul Shannon)*

The green running-in board betrays the Southern origins of the rather forlorn branch terminus at Gunnislake, cut back from Callington in 1966. Waiting for custom in this view dated 15 September 1973 is a Class 118 twin set comprising cars W51311 and W51326. At least one gas lamp appears to be still in service on the platform. *(David Rapson)*

services to the ferry terminal ceased in September 1987. The rails then remained in place and were last used by a railtour in 1999. Demolition finally took place in autumn 2020.

The coastal branches to Bridport and Swanage survived into the 1970s. Bridport had been proposed for closure in the Beeching Report and it was only thanks to effective local lobbying that it survived as long as it did. Its stations became unstaffed in 1969, which helped to reduce costs, and for a time its outlook seemed positive. However, BR made a fresh closure application in 1971 and on this occasion local resistance proved futile. The branch closed in May 1975 and the permanent way was quickly dismantled. The Swanage branch was different insofar as it was not mentioned in the Beeching Report. However, in 1967 BR announced its intention to close the line and, after a delay caused by concerns about replacement bus services, the last BR train to Swanage left Wareham on 1 January 1972. The route immediately became a target for preservation and today the Swanage Railway runs a successful heritage operation between Swanage and Norden. A signalled connection with the national network just outside Wareham was restored in 2007, making it possible to run through trains.

The 24¾-mile branch from Taunton to Minehead tells another story with a happy ending. Despite a healthy volume of traffic, the line was listed for closure in the Beeching Report and BR services ended in January 1971. However, the track was left in place and within a few months the West Somerset Railway Company set about the task of bringing it back to life. A public service between Minehead and Blue Anchor began in March 1976 and operations were extended to Blue Anchor three years later. After many setbacks, the main-line connection at Norton Fitzwarren was finally restored, initially for occasional specials and then in 2006 with appropriate signalling for regular services to and from Network Rail.

Secondary routes that have never seriously been proposed for closure include Castle Cary-Yeovil-Weymouth and Bath-Westbury-Salisbury. The first of these lines is single-track as far as Dorchester with loops at Yeovil Pen Mill and Maiden Newton. An island of mechanical signalling survives at Pen Mill, surrounded by power boxes at Westbury, Exeter, Salisbury and Dorchester. The service frequency today is roughly two-hourly, with most trains running between Gloucester and Weymouth. The Bath-Salisbury line is double-track throughout and was

The line from Crediton to Coleford Junction changed from a double-track line to two independent single lines in 1971, one leading to Okehampton and the other to Barnstaple. A Class 101 unit with cars W51523, W59551 and W51452 takes the Barnstaple line as it leaves Crediton on 19 September 1974. The unit had not long been transferred from Scotland and repainted blue and grey. *(David Rapson)*

fully re-signalled by the 1980s. The service on this route has increased dramatically from nine weekday trains in each direction in 1973 to more than thirty today. North of Westbury, the Trowbridge-Thingley Junction link reopened for seasonal passenger services in 1975 and all the year round in 1976; its intermediate station at Melksham reopened in 1985. The line now sees a roughly two-hourly service between Westbury and Swindon.

In the Bristol area, the Beeching Report foresaw the closure of all branch and secondary lines, leaving just the ex-GWR main lines to Taunton, Bath and Filton and the ex-Midland route to Yate via Mangotsfield. In the event, BR dispensed with the ex-Midland line in 1969 by diverting its trains via Filton. Conversely, the branch from Bristol to Severn Beach via Avonmouth survived the threat of closure and remains in use today, albeit in much simplified form. In 1973, BR ran an approximately hourly service between Bristol and Severn Beach, with some additional peak-hour trains. Today, Great Western Railway maintains a half-hourly frequency as far as Avonmouth, with alternate trains and some peak-hour extras continuing to Severn Beach. With one passing loop at Clifton Down and a short double-track section at Avonmouth, there is little room for manoeuvre in the timetable. The line is set to receive a boost with the planned opening of Portway park and ride station, under construction since 2019.

Local services on main lines have benefited from several station openings and re-openings. A new Filton Abbey Wood station opened in March 1996 to replace Filton, which retained a minimal service until May 1997. On the Bristol Parkway-Gloucester line, Yate gained a new station in May 1989 and Cam & Dursley in May 1994. Ashchurch lost its station in November 1971, but new platforms were brought into use in June 1997. However, Pilning station, which handled just two westbound and three eastbound trains each weekday in 1973, has faded further into obscurity since the footbridge giving access to its westbound platform was removed in 2016; it currently receives only two calls a week, both on Saturdays.

Some trains on the Barnstaple branch were still locomotive-hauled in the 1980s, generally using Class 31 traction. 31135 waits to set off with the 1410 from Barnstaple to Exeter St Davids on 31 July 1982. Sister locomotive 31416 was also working the branch on that day. Barnstaple signal box and its associated signals were decommissioned in 1987, after which the line was controlled remotely from Crediton. *(Paul Shannon)*

The vacant trackbed and abandoned platform recall busier times at Exmouth, as a hybrid Class 118/101 set comprising cars W51311, W59538 and W51326 waits to depart with the 1422 to Exeter Central on 1 June 1976. The track layout had been rationalised in 1968 and the one remaining line was shortened in 1975. *(David Rapson)*

The Southern Region green totem contrasts with the two Western Region Class 118 DMUs in this scene at Weymouth on 26 October 1977. On the right, cars W51304, W59471 and W51319 wait to depart with a cross-country train to Bristol via Westbury, while on the left cars W51302, W59469 and W51317 tick over between duties. *(Paul Shannon)*

Just weeks before the end of regular trains on the unique Weymouth tramway, Class 438 unit 8030 departs from Weymouth Quay with the 1855 boat train to London Waterloo on 28 July 1987. Propulsion from the rear is provided by 33113. By that time this was the only scheduled train of the day from Weymouth Quay, connecting out of a morning sailing from Jersey and Guernsey. *(David J. Hayes)*

A Class 119 cross-country DMU comprising cars W51090, W59421 and W51062 calls at Yeovil Pen Mill with a Weymouth-bound service on 25 October 1977. The unusual station layout with two platform faces flanking the Up line is accompanied by a bustling goods yard, dealing with steel plate and sugar beet among other cargoes. Yeovil Pen Mill was partially resignalled in 2009, but the main change was replacing some of the lower quadrant semaphores with upper quadrants and the station remains an island of mechanical signalling today. *(Paul Shannon)*

The ex-LSWR main line from Salisbury to Exeter was downgraded to secondary status in 1967. Most of it was reduced to single track and a number of intermediate stations were closed. In the mid-1970s the line supported a roughly two-hourly service between London Waterloo and Exeter St Davids, with most trains calling at most stations, plus a number of shorter-distance workings. 33014 heads west near Yeovil with the 1300 Waterloo-Exeter service on 28 August 1978. Locomotive haulage remained a feature of the line until the 1990s, when Class 159 units took over. *(David Rapson)*

The Southern Region Class 33s reached Western Region metals via Westbury as well as via Yeovil. 33002 passes Hanging Langford, between Salisbury and Westbury, with the 1310 Portsmouth Harbour-Bristol Temple Meads train on 21 August 1987. The train comprises mainly Mark 1 stock but includes a Mark 2 brake first corridor in the middle. The Portsmouth-Bristol-Cardiff service switched to diesel units, initially Class 155s, in May 1988. *(Paul Shannon)*

In the late 1980s Class 50s regularly hauled local trains between Taunton and Bristol alongside their remaining InterCity duties. 50014 *Warspite* heads north near Highbridge with the 1900 Taunton-Bristol Temple Meads train on 28 July 1987. The locomotive was withdrawn just under five months later. *(Paul Shannon)*

Although Bristol and Avonmouth were both important locations, the railway linking them was a single-track line which carried only the modest Bristol-Severn Beach passenger service. Most freight to and from Avonmouth used the Filton line instead. Ambling along near Redland on 20 June 1974 is Class 121 car W55033 with the 0800 from Bristol Temple Meads to Severn Beach. *(David Rapson)*

Hallen Marsh Junction marks the convergence of the freight-only line from Filton and the Bristol-Severn Beach branch. The area offered a feast of semaphore signalling with five boxes in quick succession until the modernisation of January 1988. Class 117 cars W51352 and W51394 flank Class 101 trailer W59539 on an afternoon working to Severn Beach in 1986. *(Michael Rhodes)*

The Swindon-Cheltenham line was a double-track main line until 1968, when BR singled the 12-mile section between Swindon and Kemble. The line then became more of a secondary route, with a limited number of through workings to and from London. A Class 101 set comprising cars W51462, W59530 and W51530 calls at Kemble with a train for Swindon on 31 August 1981. On the right is the rump of the former Cirencester branch, which closed to passengers in 1964. Network Rail restored the double track between Swindon and Kemble in 2014 to give greater flexibility in the timetable. *(Paul Shannon)*

CHAPTER 2

LONDON AND THE SOUTH EAST

London's railway network has always been naturally dominated by radial routes from central termini to the suburbs and beyond. However, even within a few miles of Trafalgar Square there are local lines that do not follow that pattern. Some of those lines faced a real closure threat in the 1960s but have since been transformed into busy urban arteries.

The North London Line has seen a huge upturn in its fortunes in the last half century. Although electrified by the LNWR in 1916, the section from Camden Road to Richmond via Gospel Oak was earmarked for closure in the Beeching Report, leaving Broad Street with only a modified service to Watford Junction via Primrose Hill. However, the Richmond line survived; it carried a 20-minute interval off-peak service in 1973, with some morning peak extras from Willesden Junction to Broad Street. There were also eleven peak-only trains from Watford Junction to Broad Street via Primrose Hill and eight peak-only trains from ex-Great Northern metals via Finsbury Park. The latter trains stopped running in 1976 when the Great Northern suburban line was electrified and its suburban services diverted to Moorgate.

The first stage of a North London Line revival was the reopening of the Dalston-Stratford line to passengers in 1979, with diesel units running between Camden Road and North Woolwich via Dalston and Stratford. Intermediate stations were opened at Hackney Wick and Hackney Central in 1980, Dalston Kingsland in 1983 and Homerton in 1985. Third-rail electrification was extended from Dalston to North Woolwich in

A Class 501 set with cars M61153, M70153 and M75153 calls at South Acton with a morning North London Line train from Richmond to Broad Street on 7 March 1978. All Class 501 stock had window bars to prevent passengers from leaning out in Hampstead Tunnel with its limited clearance. *(David Rapson)*

The Class 501 sets carried blue and grey livery in their later years. Cars M75171, M70167 and M61151 form an afternoon train to Richmond on 1 July 1983. The location is Kensal Green Junction, where the line from Gospel Oak splits three ways – to Willesden yards and the West Coast Main Line on the left, to Willesden Junction High Level in the middle and to Willesden Junction Low Level on the right. The area was resignalled in 1985. *(Paul Shannon)*

1985, which enabled BR to divert Richmond trains to North Woolwich instead of Broad Street. That change left Broad Street with only the peak-hour service from Watford Junction; clearly, the days of the once-busy City terminus were numbered and it closed completely on the evening of 27 June 1986. By way of compensation, the Watford Junction trains were diverted into Liverpool Street via a new curve at Hackney, but that arrangement did not last long and the service was withdrawn in September 1992.

Today, the central section of the North London Line between Willesden and Stratford is part of London Overground and supports an intensive service of eight trains an hour in each direction, running alternately to and from Richmond and Clapham Junction. Additionally, although no trace remains of Broad Street – indeed there was not much left of it during its last years of operation – the trackbed from Dalston towards Broad Street now sees trains once again since the opening of the East London Line extension in 2010.

The North Woolwich branch has had a varied history. It was spared by the recommendations of the Beeching Report and continued to host a local service from Tottenham Hale via Stratford. However, the line was increasingly neglected and by 1972 the section beyond Custom House was effectively a long siding terminating at a single platform at North Woolwich. Closure was now a distinct possibility. Then in May 1985 the line's fortunes began to improve. The section from Stratford to North Woolwich was electrified to form part of the extended North London Line and through trains began operating between Richmond and North Woolwich.

This development left the Tottenham Hale-Stratford service as an isolated stretch of diesel operation, with only a limited rush-hour service. Not surprisingly, that service was withdrawn in July 1985 and the single intermediate station at Lea Bridge was closed. The line, however, provided a useful through route between the Lea Valley Line and Stratford, and it was electrified in 1989 to cater for a new service to and from Cambridge. A new

Refurbished Southern Region Class 416 units took over North London Line services from Richmond in 1985, allowing the withdrawal of the 29-year-old Class 501s. Unit 6316 approaches Camden Road station with the 0824 Richmond-North Woolwich train on 4 November 1988. The left-hand route behind the train is the link to Primrose Hill, which was used by Watford trains until their withdrawal in September 1992. *(Paul Shannon)*

Cravens Class 105 units were the mainstay of the Camden Road-North Woolwich service when it started in 1979. Cars E53365 and E54126 have just left Stratford Low Level station with the 1158 from Camden Road on 18 February 1985. The conductor rail is already in place for the electric service which would begin later that year. Stratford Southern signal box closed in 1984 and was later preserved – without its supporting girder structure – on the Mid Norfolk Railway. *(Paul Shannon)*

Despite having been electrified in 1985, the North Woolwich branch remained a quaint railway backwater. Class 416 unit 6309 calls at Silvertown with the 1535 North Woolwich-Richmond train on 4 July 1989. The track on the right was an independent single line from Canning Town giving access to a scrapyard on the Silvertown Tramway. *(Paul Shannon)*

Birmingham Class 104 cars M53501 and M53453 pass Junction Road Junction with the 1315 Gospel Oak-Barking service on 6 August 1985. Behind the photographer is the junction for Kentish Town and the Midland Main Line, which was used by Barking trains until their diversion to Gospel Oak in 1981. The semaphores were removed when the area was resignalled in November 1985. *(Paul Shannon)*

The new Barking Riverside branch leaves the Tilbury line by means of a flyover across Ripple Lane yard. The whole branch is elevated, including the two-platform Riverside terminus. Unit 710273 comes off the long viaduct at Ripple Lane with the 1748 Barking Riverside-Gospel Oak working on 25 July 2022. On the adjacent track 66084 edges forward with a scrap metal train for Immingham. *(Paul Shannon)*

station at Lea Bridge opened in May 2016 and today it is served by four trains an hour in each direction – far more than BR ever ran.

Further change for the North Woolwich branch came in December 2006, when the North London Line service was cut back to Stratford. The trackbed between Stratford and Canning Town was reused for an extension of the Docklands Light Railway, which opened in 2011. The formation between Custom House and North Woolwich was abandoned. However, part of that formation was later followed by the Elizabeth Line, which carried its first passengers in May 2022. The Elizabeth Line includes a new station at Custom House, adjacent to the site of the pre-2006 station, but it dives underground just before reaching the site of North Woolwich station.

The Gospel Oak-Barking line is another orbital route that has recovered from the doldrums. In the 1960s it carried a local passenger service between Kentish Town and Barking, with a few trains running through to or from St Pancras. It was targeted for closure in the Beeching Report but survived, albeit in an increasingly run-down state. In 1973 BR ran a basically hourly service between Kentish Town and Barking, with some additional peak trains. In 1981 the service was diverted to a new platform at Gospel Oak instead of Kentish Town as a result of the electrification and upgrading of the Midland Main Line.

From 1981 the Gospel Oak-Barking line remained an island of diesel operation, using various types of units, until its electrification was finally completed in

The 'Kenny Belle' peak-hour trains between Kensington Olympia and Clapham Junction used a wide variety of stock in the 1980s, including Class 73 electro-diesels coupled to an unpowered Class 438 (4TC) unit. 73112 passes Earls Court with unit 8018 forming the 1625 from Clapham Junction on 1 September 1989. Despite its InterCity livery, 73112 was allocated to Network SouthEast at that time. *(Paul Shannon)*

2018. Once sufficient rolling-stock became available, the service frequency was increased to four trains an hour. Further investment saw the line extended by 2¾ miles at its eastern end to a new terminus at Barking Riverside, serving a former industrial area undergoing regeneration. The Riverside extension opened on 18 July 2022.

The West London Line has similarly been transformed from a quiet backwater to a busy artery for local passenger traffic. In the early 1970s the only BR trains using Kensington Olympia station were the rush-hour shuttle to and from Clapham Junction, remarkable for its use of locomotive and stock, and long-distance Motorail services. The latter ceased in 1981. However, BR added Kensington Olympia to the InterCity map in 1986, with long-distance trains avoiding the London termini to provide links between Northern England, the Midlands and the South Coast. The InterCity service continued until 2008, albeit much diminished towards the end.

Meanwhile, the potential of the West London line for local traffic began to be realised, with the introduction of an all-day service between Willesden Junction and Clapham Junction via Olympia in 1994. New intermediate stations were opened at West Brompton in 1999, Shepherds Bush in 2008 and Imperial Wharf in 2009. Today, Kensington Olympia is served not only by four off-peak trains an hour between Stratford and Clapham Junction but also by hourly trains between Watford Junction and East Croydon.

Elsewhere in Greater London – and just across the border into neighbouring counties – some non-radial local lines have survived while others faced the axe. On the Western Region, the branches to Staines West

Uniquely on the British railway network, the Greenford branch service terminates in a bay sandwiched between the two London Underground Central line platforms. Class 121 car W55028 has just arrived at Greenford with the 1055 from Ealing Broadway on 27 December 1984. Today, the service runs between Greenford and West Ealing and uses Class 165 stock. *(Paul Shannon)*

and Uxbridge Vine Street were early casualties of the Beeching period, but the West Ealing-Greenford line survived and supports a half-hourly all-day service today. On the London Midland Region, the short branch to Belmont closed in 1964, while even the radial routes out of Marylebone faced the threat of closure in the 1980s, thankfully averted given the growth of traffic at Marylebone in recent years. On the Eastern Region, the Palace Gates branch closed in 1964, but the Romford-Upminster line – a strangely rural route through a densely populated area – resisted the axe and was electrified in 1986. The branches to Chingford and Enfield Town were never seriously threatened.

South of the Thames, the Beeching Report foresaw only one suburban closure, the 2½-mile Woodside-Selsdon line. That line actually survived until 1983, by which time Selsdon was one of the last stations in the country to be lit entirely by gas. The neighbouring branch to Addiscombe continued to operate with a half-hourly off-peak service and some peak-hour extras, but it gradually declined and ended up as a single-track railway serving unstaffed stations. It closed in May 1997, after which some of the formation was reused by Croydon Tramlink.

Although not listed in the Beeching Report, the Wimbledon-West Croydon line was a largely single-track non-radial route which struggled to maintain passenger numbers. It closed at the same time as the Addiscombe branch in May 1997 and the track was also incorporated into Croydon Tramlink, reopening for business in May 2000.

Moving away from London, the rail network has lost some of its branch lines, but many have survived. In the Thames Valley, the 2¾-mile branch to Windsor & Eton Central carries a slightly more frequent service than it did 50 years ago, but without the occasional through trains to or from Paddington. The frequency of the Maidenhead-Bourne End-Marlow service is much the same as in the early 1970s, but again without the through Paddington trains. However, the link from Bourne End to High Wycombe closed in May 1970, despite not having been listed in the Beeching Report. The 4½-mile Henley-on-Thames branch repeats the pattern, with more frequent trains but no through working onto the main line.

In Oxfordshire, the Abingdon branch lost its regular passenger service in 1963, but the short branch from Radley remained open for freight and excursion traffic until the 1980s. The single-track line from Oxford to Princes Risborough also closed to passengers in 1963, its potential use as an alternative Oxford-London corridor never having been realised.

The line from Oxford to Bicester, forming part of the one-time Oxford-Cambridge route, has seen a gradual recovery since the grim days of the 1960s. While the Beeching Report envisaged retaining the whole line, BR proposed its closure to passengers in 1964 and the section from Oxford to Bicester and Bletchley was duly axed in 1967. However, the track remained in place for freight, and local services resumed between Oxford and Bicester in May 1989. The line then found an enhanced role in 2015, when a new curve between the Chiltern Line and the Oxford-Bicester line enabled through running between Marylebone and Oxford. Work to restore the railway between Bicester and Bletchley began in 2020.

Around Aylesbury, the single-track link from Princes Risborough enjoys a much better service today than it did in the early 1970s. It now carries one train an hour between Marylebone and Aylesbury throughout the day, whereas 50 years ago it was only

The Wimbledon-Sutton line still had a branch-line feel in the early 1980s with mechanical signalling much in evidence. Class 414 units 5616 and 5632 form a midday departure from Wimbledon on 21 September 1981. The area was resignalled in the following year with the closure of Wimbledon 'B' and 'C' boxes as well as those at St Helier, Sutton, Mitcham, Mitcham Junction, Beddington Lane and Waddon Marsh. *(Paul Shannon)*

The former LSWR branch to Windsor & Eton Riverside was electrified in 1930 as part of a large-scale programme to extend the third rail to outer suburban and long-distance routes. Class 455 unit 5832 calls at Datchet with the 1140 Windsor & Eton Riverside-Waterloo service on 20 February 1986. At that time the branch supported a weekday off-peak service of two trains an hour, just as it does today. *(Paul Shannon)*

In contrast to the ex-LSWR branch, the former GWR branch to Windsor & Eton Central has remained diesel-worked. Class 121 car W55027 waits at the single-platform terminus before forming the 1208 Windsor & Eton Central-Slough train on 20 February 1986. By that time the former rush-hour through trains to and from Paddington had ceased and the branch operation was entirely self-contained. *(Paul Shannon)*

The modest and rather unappealing 1960s terminus at Marlow is pictured in Network SouthEast days, as Class 101 cars 51208 and 54402 arrive with the 1642 service from Maidenhead on 4 August 1993. This was one of the last first-generation DMUs to operate in the Thames Valley, as the takeover by Class 165 Networker units was well under way. *(Paul Shannon)*

The Brunel era station building and adjacent Oxford Canal provide an attractive setting for Class 121 car W55027 as it calls at Heyford with the 1707 Banbury-Oxford service on 8 April 1983. The building was scheduled for demolition in the 1980s but was fortunately rescued for eventual reconstruction at the Didcot Railway Centre. *(Paul Shannon)*

The one-time main line through Princes Risborough was downgraded in the 1960s and singled between Princes Risborough and Aynho Junction. The Down platform at Princes Risborough was taken out of use and all through trains, including those between Marylebone and the Aylesbury branch, had to call at the former Up platform. A four-car Class 115 set is signalled for the Aylesbury line at Princes Risborough on 20 August 1986. The station area was resignalled in 1991 and a new Down platform was provided in 1998, while the line to Aynho Junction was redoubled in two stages in 1998 and 2002. *(Paul Shannon)*

served during the peak hours and in the late evening. North of Aylesbury, a short length of passenger railway was restored as far as Aylesbury Vale Parkway in December 2008.

On former LNWR metals, the branches from Watford Junction to both Croxley Green and St Albans Abbey faced closure in the 1960s. Efforts were made to keep the Croxley Green service going, including an experimental all-day service which ran briefly in the late 1980s. However, traffic levels failed to improve, and the branch carried its last revenue-earning trains in March 1996. Its permanent closure was confirmed in 2003, albeit with the faint hope that one day the alignment might return to use as an extension of the Metropolitan Line. The St Albans Abbey branch fared better. It was electrified in 1988 and currently supports a 45-minute interval service on weekdays, the highest frequency that can be achieved given that the line has no passing loop.

In the Bletchley area, the Newport Pagnell branch closed in 1964, while the Bletchley-Bedford line was the only part of the Oxford-Cambridge route to escape closure in 1967. A further attempt to withdraw the Bletchley-Bedford service was made in 1971 and that proposal was approved in the following year; however, it survived again and received a boost in 1984 when trains were diverted from the run-down remains of Bedford St Johns to the Midland Main Line station in Bedford. Today's hourly interval timetable is similar to that of the early 1970s.

In central Hertfordshire, the former Great Northern branch from Welwyn Garden City to Dunstable via Luton Bute Street closed to passengers in 1965. On ex-Great

Eastern territory, the Buntingford branch closed in 1964, while the Hertford East branch has survived into the twenty-first century, despite proposals in the 1970s to convert part of it into a road.

The branch lines of Essex include several commuter routes which have thrived in recent decades with the general increase in commuting distances to London. The service on the Upminster-Grays line in the mid-1980s consisted mainly of a shuttle between Upminster and Tilbury, but today the line supports an off-peak service of two trains an hour between Fenchurch Street and Southend Central. The Southminster branch was electrified in 1986 and now benefits from some peak-hour trains to and from Liverpool Street as well as an hourly Wickford-Southminster shuttle during the day. The Braintree branch survived the threat of closure in the 1960s and was significantly upgraded in the 1970s, with re-signalling and electrification as well as the raising and lengthening of station platforms. Today, most of the hourly trains from Braintree run through to Liverpool Street.

The Sudbury branch on the Essex/Suffolk border survived several closure attempts in the 1960s and 1970s; it is still alive today and served by an hourly train from Marks Tey. A new single-platform terminus at Sudbury opened in 1991 to allow redevelopment of the previous station site. Two other Essex branches were less fortunate: Maldon and Brightlingsea both lost their passenger services in 1964.

Essex gained a new branch line in March 1991 when BR opened a 3½-mile spur from the Liverpool Street-Cambridge line to Stansted Airport, coinciding with the completion of the airport's new terminal building. Today, Stansted Airport station sees an average of four departures an hour, including an hourly off-peak service to Norwich and a two-hourly service to Birmingham as well as regular trains to Liverpool Street.

The 'B9' headcode on Class 501 car M61163 confirms that this arrival at Watford Junction on the evening of 16 April 1981 has come from Croxley Green. At that time the branch shuttle ran at frequent intervals in the morning and evening peaks. The Class 501s on Euston-Watford and Croxley Green services were replaced by Class 313 units in 1985. *(Paul Shannon)*

The St Albans Abbey branch was reduced to a long siding from Watford in the 1960s with the closure of Bricket Wood loop. Paytrain operation began in 1966. Cravens Class 105 cars M50393 and M56120 approach the terminus with an afternoon train from Watford Junction on 18 April 1981. This scene would be transformed in 1988 by overhead electrification. *(Paul Shannon)*

Across northern Kent, the Beeching Report left the rail network virtually unscathed. The main change of the last 50 years has been the modernisation of stations and the replacement of mechanical signalling on secondary lines such as Strood-Paddock Wood and Ashford-Canterbury West-Minster. Today, the only location in northern Kent where passenger trains pass semaphore signals is Deal, on the Ramsgate-Dover line. The Sheerness branch sees a more frequent service than it did 50 years ago, but the through trains to and from Victoria no longer run.

In the southern half of the county, the Ashford-Ore (Hastings) line was targeted for closure in the Beeching Report, together with its offshoot to New Romney. While the New Romney branch with its thirteen manned level crossings closed in 1967, the Ashford-Ore line defied several closure attempts and is still going strong today, with hourly trains running mostly between Ashford and Eastbourne. The stretch between Appledore and Ore was singled in 1979 with a passing loop at Rye.

With its strong emphasis on commuter services, the rail network of Surrey has seen relatively modest change in the last half century. Virtually all lines were electrified by the 1960s, although one notable exception was the cross-country Reading-Redhill line, which is still diesel-worked today. The extension from Redhill to Tonbridge was electrified in 1993 for Channel Tunnel trains. As for the Surrey commuter branches, Epsom Downs has seen the biggest change as its original nine-platform station had shrunk to just two platforms by 1972. The reason was the loss of race traffic. A new single-platform terminus was provided at Epsom Downs in 1989, which is adequate for today's 30-minute frequency service. The nearby terminus at Tattenham Corner has seen a less severe but nonetheless significant pruning from seven platforms to three.

The Bedford-Bletchley line outlived the demise of Cambridge-Oxford services in 1967 but remained under threat in the 1970s and received little investment. The unusual open signal frame at Millbrook is pictured on 28 July 1981, with Class 25 loco 25158 piloting failed Class 105 cars M50387 and M56149 on a train for Bletchley. The line was finally resignalled in 2004, with control passing to a new signalling centre at Ridgmont. *(Paul Shannon)*

The first Vivarail Class 230 units entered passenger service with West Midlands Trains on the Bedford-Bletchley line on 23 April 2019. A pool of three units covered two regular diagrams with one unit spare. 230004 calls at Ridgmont with the 1455 Bedford-Bletchley train on 11 May 2019. Amid the background clutter is the rather fine 'cottage orné' style station building, which now houses a heritage centre with museum and gift shop. *(Paul Shannon)*

A searchlight-type signal guards the exit from the southernmost platform at Hertford East, as Class 305 unit 419 pulls out of the station after working the 1249 from Liverpool Street on 23 August 1988. The signal box dated back to 1887 and remained in use until 2003. It has since been dismantled for reinstallation on the Wensleydale Railway, also providing space for a platform extension at Hertford East. *(Paul Shannon)*

When the Stansted Airport branch opened in 1991, a dedicated fleet of five Class 322 units worked the Stansted Express service to and from Liverpool Street. These units were succeeded by Class 317s, and then by Class 379s, until a new fleet of Class 745 Flirt units entered service in 2020. Arriving at Stansted Airport on 21 March 2018 is an eight-car Class 379 formation, with unit 379029 closest to the camera. *(Paul Shannon)*

Ockendon was the only intermediate station on the Upminster-Grays line until the opening of Chafford Hundred station in 1995. Ockendon retains the only passing loop on the single-track line. Unit 357228 calls at Ockendon with the 1550 from Fenchurch Street to Southend Central on 18 April 2003. *(Paul Shannon)*

The Southminster branch has benefited from the gradual increase in commuting distances into London. Its electrification in 1986 eliminated a diesel island in this part of Essex. Unit 315802 waits at Southminster after arriving with the 1333 from Liverpool Street on 16 April 2003. At that time the station had no ticket office, but the building escaped dereliction by housing a café, an information point and a cycle hire centre. *(Paul Shannon)*

The Sheerness branch was electrified in the late 1950s and the track was doubled as far as Swale. Class 414 (2HAP) units 6131 and 6129 head south between Swale and Kemsley with an afternoon service from Sheerness on 10 June 1981. At that time the hourly local service between Sheerness and Sittingbourne was still complemented by peak-hour through trains to and from London. *(Paul Shannon)*

With the well-known Grade II listed windmill visible in the background, Class 205 (3H) unit 1111 calls at Rye with the 0812 Ashford-Hastings train on 25 August 1983. The northbound platform is out of sight behind the photographer. The former South Eastern Railway signal box was Grade II listed in 2013 and remains in use today, controlling the passing loop and level crossing. *(Paul Shannon)*

The decades of decline at Epsom Downs are all too evident in this view dated 21 September 1981, as Class 405 (4SUB) unit 4754 departs for London Victoria. The box was due to close in 1982, but a fire hastened its demise in November 1981. The whole station was replaced by a new single-platform facility in 1989. *(Paul Shannon)*

The network of rural lines in Sussex shrank considerably in the 1960s. Passenger closures between 1963 and 1969 included Haywards Heath-Horsted Keynes, Guildford-Horsham, Eridge-Hailsham-Polegate, Horsham-Shoreham-by-Sea, Groombridge-East Grinstead-Three Bridges and Uckfield-Lewes. The closure of the Uckfield-Lewes link in 1969 was a controversial one and vigorous campaigning started almost straight away to reopen it; however, some of the route has now been built over. The Tunbridge Wells-Groombridge-Eridge link managed to survive until July 1985, after which the Spa Valley Railway was able to move in and set up a heritage operation.

Of the Sussex branches and secondary routes that remain, East Grinstead was re-signalled and electrified in 1987, while the Uckfield branch was re-signalled and partly singled in 1990, and its terminus was re-sited to allow the closure of a level crossing in 1991. Along the coast, the branches to Seaford via Newhaven, Littlehampton and Bognor Regis are all well served today, the last two being remarkable for their surviving semaphore signals.

In Hampshire, the Hayling Island branch ceased operation in 1963. The lines from Poole to Salisbury and to Brockenhurst via Ringwood closed to passengers in 1964, as did the Romsey-Andover line. The Fawley branch lost its passenger service in 1966. The Alton-Winchester line lasted until February 1973, much of it later being revived as the Watercress Line heritage operation. On the Isle of Wight, the Beeching Report proposed the closure of both remaining lines, from Ryde to Ventnor and Smallbrook Junction to Newport. In the event, determined campaigning saved the main portion of the Ventnor line between Ryde and Shanklin, and this portion was electrified in 1967.

Another survivor in Hampshire is the 5-mile branch from Brockenhurst to Lymington Pier. This line holds the distinction of having been the last steam-worked branch line on BR, and an ex-LMS tank engine performed the last ever steam run-round movement at a BR branch terminus on 2 April 1967. Electric units then took over on the branch shuttle, just as they did on the main line to Bournemouth.

As with its neighbour Epsom Downs, Tattenham Corner station once had numerous platforms for racecourse traffic. Only three platform faces remained in use by August 1979, when a pair of Class 416 (2EPB) units was recorded setting out for Charing Cross. The platform end semaphores had already given way to colour lights, but Tattenham Corner retained its signal box until September 1983. *(Brian Denton)*

To enable the introduction of Paytrain operation on the Reading-Redhill-Tonbridge line, BR created a pool of through-gangwayed 3R (later Class 206) units by combining two former 6S Hastings cars with one former 2EPB driving trailer. They were nicknamed 'Tadpoles' because of the contrast between the narrow-bodied 6S vehicles and the standard-width 2EPB vehicles. Class 206 unit 1203 calls at North Camp with a Reading-bound service on 6 March 1976. *(David Rapson)*

While most trains on the East Grinstead and Uckfield branches were formed of diesel-electric units, a few peak-hour trains ran with locomotive and stock. 33007 approaches Crowborough with the 1720 from London Bridge to Uckfield on 25 August 1983. This regular duty finished in 1984, although hauled trains appeared later for a short time when there was a shortage of units. *(Paul Shannon)*

Tunbridge Wells West came close to losing its passenger service in the 1960s but actually survived until July 1985, albeit by then eking out a precarious existence with life-expired infrastructure. Class 207 (3D) unit 1305 arrives with the 0937 Eridge-Tonbridge train on 23 August 1983. On the left is Tunbridge Wells West 'A' box, which controlled movements at the west end of the station. *(Paul Shannon)*

Now flanked by high security fencing and derelict buildings, Newhaven Harbour station has survived as an intermediate call for a few trains to and from Seaford. Its neighbour Newhaven Marine was less fortunate, its closure finally having been authorised in 2020 after it lost its usable service some 14 years earlier. Unit 313214 passes through Newhaven Harbour without stopping as it forms the 1025 from Seaford to Brighton on 31 August 2022. *(Paul Shannon)*

The West Coastway line from Brighton to Portsmouth serves a string of small stations, many of which retained their manual signalling in the 1980s. Class 413 (4CAP) unit 3311 arrives at West Worthing with the 0900 Littlehampton-Brighton stopper on 27 August 1983. West Worthing signal box was decommissioned along with six others on this route in 1988. *(Paul Shannon)*

It could almost be a scene from the 1980s, but perhaps the plethora of safety notices gives the game away. Littlehampton station retains its 19th century signal box along with semaphore signals at the platform ends. Repainted in retro BR blue and grey livery, 46-year-old unit 313201 arrives with the 1505 from Bognor Regis on 31 August 2022. *(Paul Shannon)*

After Southampton Central terminus closed in 1966, the branch from Northam Junction into Southampton Eastern Docks remained in use for freight and for special trains connecting with ocean liner sailings. Electro-diesel 74001 passes Canute Road crossing on the docks branch with a Cunard boat train for Waterloo on 25 June 1977. It would have switched from diesel to electric power after joining the South Western Main Line at Northam Junction. Canute Road ground frame closed in 1981, when control passed to Eastleigh power box. *(Brian Denton)*

The 5-mile Lymington branch was electrified in 1967 at the same time as the main line to Bournemouth. Class 414 (2HAP) unit 4309, renumbered from 6078 in 1987, is pictured at Lymington Pier on 12 February 1991. This unit worked its last passenger train in 1994. Lymington later became a final outpost for slam-door stock, when South West Trains used two refurbished Class 421 (3CIG) units on the branch between 2005 and 2010. *(Brian Denton)*

On the Isle of Wight, the restricted height of Ryde Tunnel led BR to replace steam with second-hand electric units from the London Underground, dating back to the 1920s and 1930s. They were designated 4VEC (later Class 485) and 3TIS (later Class 486). Class 486 unit 031 leads a 7-car formation out of Ryde in June 1977. The use of former London Underground vehicles on the island continued with two further generations of stock: Class 483 took over in 1989 and then Class 484 – after extensive rebuilding – in 2021. *(Brian Denton)*

CHAPTER 3

EAST ANGLIA AND LINCOLNSHIRE

The network of secondary lines and branches in East Anglia had already been trimmed before the publication of the Beeching Report, but several more lines would face the axe from the mid-1960s onwards, including some which were originally considered safe.

One route which managed to survive despite its listing for closure was the 49-mile East Suffolk Line from Ipswich to Lowestoft. After its reprieve in 1966, it was essential to reduce its running costs and the first stage of this process was the de-staffing of all intermediate stations in 1967. The weekday timetable for 1973 comprised ten trains each way over the whole route, one of which was a through loco-hauled working between Liverpool Street and Lowestoft. That through service continued until May 1984.

In the early 1980s the East Suffolk Line was still double-track throughout with nine signal boxes and thirty-six public level crossings, of which twenty-five were manned. BR therefore implemented further measures to reduce costs, including the singling of the Woodbridge-Saxmundham and Halesworth-Oulton Broad North sections, the de-staffing of most level crossings and the introduction of Radio Electronic Token Block (RETB) signalling controlled from Saxmundham. The long single-track sections placed some constraints on the timetable and these were eventually eased in 2012 when Network Rail restored a passing loop at Beccles. The

In the 1980s, the Harwich branch carried a mixture of local passenger trains, boat trains and freight workings. Cravens Class 105 cars E56435 and E51262 coast into Wrabness station with the 1140 Manningtree-Harwich Town stopping train on 8 April 1983. The Harwich branch was re-signalled in 1985 and electrified in the following year. *(Paul Shannon)*

As deep-sea container traffic grew, so Felixstowe's passenger station became the poor relation of the freight business. Track alterations in 1970 created a direct link into the docks but left just a single-track spur into the unstaffed passenger terminus. With plenty of vacant land awaiting redevelopment, Class 105 cars E51293 and E54131 set out with an evening departure to Ipswich on 8 April 1983. The station buildings were saved from demolition and were later converted into a shopping centre named Great Eastern Square. *(Paul Shannon)*

RETB system was replaced by track circuit block at the same time. Today the East Suffolk Line is served by seventeen trains each way on weekdays.

The Felixstowe branch became Paytrain territory with the withdrawal of its station staff in 1966 and the terminus was reduced to a single-track stub in 1970. After that, the main change on the branch was the rapid and sustained growth of freight traffic to and from the Port of Felixstowe. It was this growth that prompted the lengthening of Derby Road loop as part of a re-signalling project in 1999, followed by the provision of a long loop at Trimley in 2019. Today, out of a weekday total of eighteen trains each way, only one pair of passenger workings is scheduled to cross at a passing loop, but crossings of passenger and freight workings are frequent and the new infrastructure has improved the reliability of all services.

The branches from Norwich to Lowestoft and Great Yarmouth have never been under serious threat. Even the remote and minuscule halt at Berney Arms, on the Reedham-Great Yarmouth line, escaped listing in the Beeching Report. Paytrain operation ousted station staff in 1967, but in many respects time stood still on those branches until 2018/19, when the semaphores finally gave way to multiple-aspect signalling. Less fortunate was the short branch from Lowestoft to Yarmouth South Town, which closed in May 1970.

The Sheringham branch is a curious amalgamation of lines built and operated by three separate railway companies. After much rationalisation, the former Midland & Great Northern Railway terminus at Cromer became an intermediate reversing point on the route to Sheringham. The onward section from Sheringham to Melton Constable closed in 1964 and

At first glance, it seems odd that Yarmouth retained both its railway routes from Norwich – via Reedham and via Acle. However, both routes were single-track and the closure of one of them would have made the pathing of trains to and from Yarmouth difficult. Class 105 cars E51293 and E54131 are about to take the Yarmouth branch at Reedham with the 0809 departure from Norwich on 17 April 1984. *(Paul Shannon)*

Anglia Railways hired preserved Class 201 Hastings unit 1001 for eleven months in 1998/99 to cover for a rolling-stock shortage. The unit worked on the Lowestoft and Yarmouth branches. It is pictured passing Whitlingham Junction with an evening working from Yarmouth on 22 August 1998. The line curving round to the left is the branch to Cromer and Sheringham. *(Michael Rhodes)*

the Norwich-Sheringham line was formally threatened with closure three years later; however, it survived and is still busy today with an approximately hourly service on weekdays. The line gained a new single-platform station at Roughton Road in 1985 and re-signalling replaced the last of the manual installations in 2000.

In central Norfolk, the network of former Great Eastern routes was substantially thinned in the 1960s. The Swaffham-Thetford and Dereham-Wells lines closed in 1964. The King's Lynn-Dereham-Wymondham line was listed for modification rather than closure in the Beeching Report, but the King's Lynn-Dereham section of that line lost its passenger service in 1968 and the remainder followed a year later. The retention of the Dereham-Wymondham line for freight traffic until the 1980s paved the way for today's heritage operation centred on Dereham.

Another late addition to the closure list was the King's Lynn-Hunstanton branch, formally proposed in 1967. Despite a rationalisation programme that included the de-staffing of stations, partial singling and the replacement of manned crossings with automatic half-barriers, the line was a big loss-maker and it closed completely in May 1969.

In Cambridgeshire, the fenland town of March has lost three of its five lines since the 1960s. First to go was the line to St Ives in 1967, although the continuation of that route from St Ives to Cambridge kept its passenger service until 1970 and remained open for freight from Fen Drayton until 1992. The March-Wisbech-Magdalen Road line followed a similar pattern; it closed to passengers in 1968, but freight traffic kept the March-Wisbech section alive until 2000. Various proposals to reopen the March-Wisbech line have so far got nowhere.

In response to long-term shortage of diesel units, Greater Anglia used DRS Class 37s and Mark 2 stock on its Yarmouth and Lowestoft routes from June 2015 until September 2019. The trains ran with two locomotives in top and tail mode, which gave better reliability than the alternative option of one locomotive and a driving van trailer. 37425 leads a Lowestoft-Norwich train past Reedham Junction, with sister locomotive 37407 at the rear. *(Michael Rhodes)*

The oddly named Shippea Hill station – there is nothing remotely resembling a hill in the area – once held the status of being Britain's least used station, with just twelve passenger journeys recorded in 2015/16. However, it handled more custom in the past and numbers have also increased again in recent years. Metro-Cammell Class 101 cars E54396 and E51221 pull away with a Norwich-bound train on 16 February 1985. The box and wooden level crossing gates remained in use until automatic barriers came into use in 2012. *(Paul Shannon)*

The March-Spalding line formed part of the Great Eastern and Great Northern Joint Line, which paralleled the East Coast Main Line and as such was regarded as strategically important. However, its passenger traffic gradually declined, and its freight carryings dwindled as well. In 1973 it still carried a good number of Summer Saturday holiday trains, but its passenger service on weekdays comprised just three trains each way. With five intermediate signal boxes and numerous level crossings it was an expensive line to operate and it closed in November 1982.

Just as in East Anglia, the Lincolnshire rail network included a lot of rural rail routes that became vulnerable as their traffic declined. The Beeching Report recommended the closure of the Peterborough-Boston-Grimsby main line as well as secondary routes from Lincoln to Boston and Firsby, Firsby to Skegness and Willoughby to Mablethorpe. The first casualty was the line from Woodhall Junction to Boston, which closed to all traffic in 1963. The Peterborough-Boston-Grimsby main line lost its passenger service and closed completely between Spalding and Louth in October 1970, and the Lincoln-Firsby and Willoughby-Mablethorpe routes were deleted from the network at the same time.

The seaside resort of Skegness was deemed worthy of a second chance and retained its rail access after 1970 by amalgamating three routes into a single branch line: the secondary route from Sleaford to Boston; a portion of the former Grimsby main line from Boston to Firsby South Junction; and the Skegness branch itself from Firsby South Junction. This amalgamation resulted in an odd-shaped line with a very sharp curve on the approach to Firsby; there were no intermediate stations between Boston and Thorpe Culvert because BR had withdrawn local services on the Grimsby line in 1961. The Skegness branch was not a high priority for modernisation and as late as 1982 there were still eight ex-Great Northern somersault signals between Boston and Skegness.

The train service to Skegness amounted to ten arrivals and eleven departures on winter weekdays in

Not for the first time, BR experimented with the idea of a four-wheeled railbus for lightly-used branch lines in the late 1970s. Consisting essentially of a Leyland bus body mounted on a specially adapted rail chassis, LEV1 was tested in East Anglia and was also exported for a time to the USA. It is pictured on one of its trial runs at Cambridge on 1 November 1980. Although LEV1 led only a short life on BR metals, it was the forerunner of the various classes of Pacer unit which entered service from the mid-1980s onwards. *(Paul Shannon)*

Local services between Bishop's Stortford and Cambridge were worked by DMUs until this stretch was electrified in 1987. Class 105 cars E51261 and E56139 arrive at Whittlesford with an afternoon stopper to Bishop's Stortford on 5 June 1981. The station goods yard was busy at that time with chemicals for Ciba-Geigy, soon to be transferred to the new Ciba-Geigy private siding at Duxford. *(Paul Shannon)*

A DMU service covered local stations between Royston and Cambridge from 1978, when electrification reached Royston, until 1988, when the final stretch to Cambridge was finally wired. Class 101 cars E56073 and E51442 pull away from bucolic Meldreth with a train for Royston – despite what the destination blind says – on 21 February 1982. Today, Meldreth has direct electric trains to London every hour in the off peak. *(Paul Shannon)*

1973, with half a dozen extras in the summer months. The extras were mostly locomotive-hauled and came from Cambridge, Leicester, Derby, Chesterfield and Sheffield. In 1977 BR reduced the opening hours of the branch to ten hours a day in order to reduce staffing costs at the numerous level crossings; this resulted in some early morning and late evening trains being replaced by buses. In 1985 the first train arrival at Skegness on winter weekdays was not until 1125 and the last departure was at 1916. A number of summer-only extras still ran.

Today, Skegness is reached by a roughly hourly service throughout the day, with all trains running to or from Nottingham. The station has four platform faces but only two are in regular use. The somersault signals on the branch have long disappeared, but mechanical signal boxes survive at Heckington, Hubberts Bridge, Boston, Bellwater Junction, Sibsey, Thorpe Culvert, Wainfleet and Skegness.

At the southern end of the Peterborough-Grimsby line, the section between Peterborough and Spalding remained open for freight after October 1970. It wasn't long before a basic passenger service on that line resumed. In a unique move at that time, two local councils agreed to fund a shuttle service of two trains a day between Peterborough and Spalding from 7 June 1971. The service was successful and gradually the line became re-established as part of the national network, albeit without its three intermediate stations which had closed in 1961. After the March-Spalding line had closed, the trains that had previously used that line were diverted via Peterborough, and by 1985 the Peterborough-Spalding line had a weekday service of seven trains each way. The separate Peterborough-Spalding shuttle continued

Is it a three- or four-car unit? The bi-mode Class 755s introduced by Greater Anglia in 2019 have a separate power pack vehicle containing their diesel engine which is much shorter than the passenger-carrying vehicles. It can be seen in front of the trailing passenger-carrying vehicle in this view of unit 755338 at Manea dated 16 July 2021. The working is the 1750 from Peterborough to Ipswich, one of the relatively few trains on this route that is booked to call at Manea. *(Paul Shannon)*

to operate alongside the longer-distance services until May 2021, when the frequency of the Peterborough-Lincoln service was increased to cover the whole day.

Two other sections of the Lincolnshire network that lost their passenger service in 1970 – Grimsby to Louth and Lincoln to Bardney – remained open for specific freight flows, but no passenger revival was in prospect and they closed in 1980 and 1981 respectively. Meanwhile the Joint Line between Spalding and Lincoln saw some enhancements with the reopening of Metheringham and Ruskington stations in 1975. Today, East Midlands Railway provides a roughly hourly service on weekdays between Peterborough, Spalding and Lincoln.

Further north, the Gainsborough-Barnetby line was still considered a trunk route in the 1960s and was not under threat. Its weekday passenger service in 1973 comprised four eastbound and five westbound trains between Sheffield and Cleethorpes, plus the overnight newspaper train from Manchester to Cleethorpes. However, its patronage declined, and so too did the state of the infrastructure. BR applied a 40mph speed limit to the line in 1981 and two sections were singled soon afterwards. Then in 1989 BR published its formal proposal to close the line. That proposal was withdrawn two years later, but the service was reduced to just three trains a day on Saturdays and none on the other days of the week from October 1993. The Saturday trains were suspended due to industrial action from August 2018 until February 2019, but from the May 2019 timetable change Gainsborough Central briefly became the terminus of an hourly six-days-a-week service from Sheffield. Unfortunately, the pandemic put an end to those trains and, when services resumed in May 2022, they were reduced to just two trains a day, six days a week, between Sheffield and Gainsborough Central, and nothing at all to Kirton Lindsey and Brigg.

The weekday service on the March-Spalding line was thin, especially after the line lost its last all-year-round long-distance working, the Harwich-Manchester boat train, in 1973. Class 114 cars E50019 and E56010 approach Grassmoor Junction, at the north end of Whitemoor yard, with the lunchtime service to Cambridge on 13 January 1981. *(Paul Shannon)*

The March-Spalding line came to life on Summer Saturdays with various holiday trains and special excursions. 31253 passes Murrow West with the 1523 Yarmouth-Sheffield holiday train on 20 June 1982. Other workings recorded that day included 40136 on Yarmouth-Newcastle, 37109 on Yarmouth-Sheffield and 25032 and 25286 on Yarmouth-Derby trains. Murrow West signal box was converted into a private dwelling after the line closed in 1982. *(Paul Shannon)*

The expansive layout at Spalding recalls busier times, as Class 105 cars E51291 and E56144 depart from the Up bay with the morning train to Peterborough on 29 October 1980. The adjacent through platform is occupied by a rake of parcels vans. Today, only two platform faces remain in use at Spalding, one bidirectional and the other for northbound trains only. *(Paul Shannon)*

Sleaford was the meeting point of the Skegness branch and the March-Doncaster line, although trains on the latter route could use the Sleaford avoiding line until the mid-1980s – and again from 2014 – instead of passing through the station. 31161 departs from Sleaford with the 0846 Sheffield-Skegness train on 31 July 1984. Sleaford boasted four signal boxes at that time, of which two – West and East – survive today. *(Paul Shannon)*

Alongside the locomotive-hauled holiday trains, lengthy DMU formations were a feature of Skegness branch operations in the 1980s. In this view dated 5 June 1982, Class 114 cars E50008 and E56019 are coupled to Class 120 cars M50714, M59293 and M50678 to form the 1139 Grantham-Skegness service. The train is running alongside the South Forty Foot Drain near Hubberts Bridge. *(David Rapson)*

The Skegness branch was unique in retaining a good number of Great Northern pattern somersault signals in the early 1980s. Two examples guard the level crossing at Havenhouse as a mixed DMU formation comprising cars E50039, E56013, M50730, M59283 and M50656 arrives with the 1344 from Skegness to Nottingham on 1 August 1981. The box closed in 1989 and the crossing was then supervised from nearby Wainfleet. *(Paul Shannon)*

A four-car DMU comprising Class 105 cars E56442 and F51281 and Class 114 cars E56028 and E50002 approaches Swinderby with a Cleethorpes-Newark train on 30 May 1980. The Class 114 cars are carrying the short-lived white and blue livery that denoted refurbished stock. The 1901-built signal box is still in use today, having outlived all others in the area. Swinderby is also the last outpost of semaphore signalling on the Lincoln-Leicester route. *(Paul Shannon)*

The Lincoln-Barnetby line is now very much a secondary route, especially since the withdrawal of the regular through trains between King's Cross and Cleethorpes in 1993. Single car 153313 rounds the curve at Pelham Street Junction as it approaches Lincoln Central with a Cleethorpes-Newark service on 1 April 2008. Trains on this route ran via Lincoln St Marks until the line between Pelham Street Junction and Boultham closed in 1985. *(Paul Shannon)*

Saxilby was the only minor station to survive the 1960s cuts on the Doncaster-Lincoln-March line. Class 114 cars E50003, E56037, E50014 and E56040 call with a Lincoln-bound train on the morning of 20 June 1981. The Derby-built Class 114 sets were the mainstay of local services in Lincolnshire for the best part of 30 years. *(Paul Shannon)*

The Gainsborough-Barnetby line still enjoyed a usable train service when Class 114 cars E50006 and E56012 were photographed leaving Kirton Lindsey with the 1653 Sheffield-Grimsby Town train on 12 April 1983. This stretch of the line had been singled earlier in the previous year to save maintenance and renewal costs. *(Paul Shannon)*

Class 31/4 locos with rakes of Mark 1 stock took over Manchester-Cleethorpes trains in the mid-1980s following the withdrawal of the Class 123 and Class 124 DMUs. The 31/4s also worked between Newark and Cleethorpes. Passing the fine array of bracket signals at Wrawby Junction on 1 August 1984 is 31425 with the 0950 from Newark Northgate to Cleethorpes. *(Paul Shannon)*

DMUs with tail traffic could still be seen in the early 1980s. Refurbished Class 114 cars E56004 and E50024 pass Garden Street crossing with a CCT parcels van in tow as they approach Grimsby Town station on 5 June 1980. Further parcels activity is visible on the left, with pilot loco 08751 coupled to a BG van on the station through line. *(Paul Shannon)*

Until the Humber Bridge opened in June 1981, ferries from Hull connected at New Holland Pier with trains to Cleethorpes and Barton-on-Humber. The northern shore of the Humber estuary is just visible through the haze as Class 105 cars E51284 and E56445 wait for custom at New Holland Pier on 5 June 1980. Both Cleethorpes and Barton-on-Humber trains used the same platform at New Holland Pier; a second platform on the west side of the station was used by motor vehicles going to and from the ferry. *(Paul Shannon)*

On South Humberside, the Beeching Report saw no future for the branch from Ulceby to New Holland Pier, nor its offshoots to Barton-on-Humber and Immingham Dock. The service to Immingham ceased in 1963, but the other lines kept going with little sign of modernisation. In 1980 the triangle at New Holland was still double-track throughout with a signal box at each of its three junctions. At least two Great Central lower quadrant semaphores remained in use. However, the triangle became redundant in 1981 when the opening of the Humber road bridge caused withdrawal of the ferry from New Holland Pier. As well as closing the Pier station, BR relocated New Holland Town station to a position beside Barrow Road crossing and introduced a direct Cleethorpes-Barton-on-Humber service. Today, East Midlands Railway maintains a weekday service of eight trains a day on that route.

CHAPTER 4

THE MIDLANDS

If the recommendations of the Beeching Report had been implemented in full, then today there would be no east-west routes connecting the East Coast and Midland main lines between Bletchley-Bedford in the south and Nottingham-Grantham in the north. Not only would secondary routes have disappeared, but the important Leicester-Peterborough line would also have been axed. In reality, good sense prevailed and Leicester-Peterborough survived, carrying a mixture of long-distance and local traffic. However, much of that line has a branch line feel to it, with nine manual signal boxes still in use between Frisby in the west and Uffington in the east.

Casualties of the 1960s cutbacks in Northamptonshire included the ex-LNWR routes from Northampton to Peterborough via Wellingborough, and from Rugby to Peterborough via Market Harborough. The ex-Midland lines from Kettering to Manton Junction and from Melton Mowbray to Nottingham also closed, although the Kettering-Manton Junction stretch remained an

Only the modern shelter on the westbound platform detracts from the steam-age feel of Lowdham station, as Class 120 cars M53663, M59121 and M53696 call with the 1420 Crewe-Cleethorpes on 30 July 1984. The signal box dating back to 1896 and its wooden crossing gates were retired from service in 2016, but the box was preserved nearby and now houses a museum with a display of Midland Railway signalling equipment. (Paul Shannon)

A three-car DMU comprising Class 120 motor vehicles M53656 and M53743 and Class 101 trailer M59531 departs from Newark Castle with the 1540 from Lincoln St Marks to Crewe on 26 July 1984. The Italianate station building, completed in 1846 and now Grade II listed, is mainly hidden by the train and by the 1950s canopy. *(Paul Shannon)*

important freight and diversionary route and has since re-joined the passenger map.

Given that Corby was one of the UK's largest population centres without a passenger station, the case for reintroducing some kind of service was strong. The first revival came in April 1987 when, with financial support from Northampton County Council and Corby District Council, BR introduced an experimental hourly service between Kettering and Corby. A simple platform was reinstated on the west side of the line. Although the service was initially well used, it ended in May 1990 after the withdrawal of financial support. Corby's second renaissance took place in 2009, when East Midlands Trains launched an hourly service to a new platform and transport interchange on the east side of the line. The line from Kettering was later redoubled and electrified, allowing a half-hourly electric service between St Pancras and Corby to start in May 2021. A small number of trains also run on the non-electrified line between Corby and Melton Mowbray.

The city of Nottingham suffered several passenger route losses in the 1960s, including the former Great Central Main Line from Leicester to Staveley and beyond, the former Great Northern lines to Pinxton and Derby Friargate, and the former Midland line to Mansfield and Worksop. However, the ex-Midland line to Newark Castle and Lincoln survived despite its listing in the Beeching Report. Indeed, the Newark-Lincoln section of that line became more important when London-Grimsby trains were routed over it following the closure of the Peterborough-Boston-Grimsby line. Local services between Nottingham and Lincoln went over to Paytrain operation in 1969, which helped to contain the costs of the small intermediate stations, but the re-signalling of the line was piecemeal. Six mechanical boxes between Nottingham and Newark survived until 2016 and Swinderby box is still in use today.

The fact that large sections of the Nottingham-Mansfield-Worksop line remained open for freight enabled the return of passenger trains on that line in

The Robin Hood line through Whitwell has seen three distinct phases: passenger and freight until 1964; freight only from 1964 till 1998; and then mainly passenger with occasional and diminishing freight from 1998 onwards. Central Trains unit 156408 has just called at Whitwell with an afternoon Worksop-Nottingham train on 16 July 2007. The derelict land on the right was once occupied by Whitwell Colliery sidings. *(Paul Shannon)*

the 1990s. Mansfield in particular had held the unenviable status as the largest town without a railway station. The first stage of the reopening used existing tracks from Nottingham to Newstead and went live in May 1993. The second stage from Newstead to Mansfield Woodhouse opened in November 1995; this stage was trickier because it required the digging out of the ex-Midland Annesley Tunnel and the building of a new connection with the former Great Northern route through Kirkby-in-Ashfield. The third and final stage covered the existing freight route from Mansfield Woodhouse to Worksop, which regained its passenger service in May 1998. Today, East Midlands Railway runs an hourly service between Nottingham and Worksop, with some peak-hour extras between Nottingham and Mansfield Woodhouse.

In North Derbyshire, the Hope Valley line faced a gloomy outlook in the 1960s, but as things turned out the axe fell instead on two neighbouring Pennine crossings – Woodhead and Buxton-Matlock – and the Hope Valley route became the principal axis linking Manchester and Sheffield. In 1969 the Hope Valley gained half a dozen St Pancras-Manchester expresses diverted from the Matlock route, and in the following year it picked up an hourly fast service between Sheffield and Manchester following the closure of Woodhead. Meanwhile, the local stations in the Hope Valley continued to be served by stopping trains between Sheffield and New Mills Central. Today, the local trains form through workings to and from Manchester and the line is used by long-distance services operated by both East Midlands Railway and Transpennine Express. Mechanical signal

For many years the Hope Valley Line was mainly a local route, with passenger expresses going either via Woodhead or on the Chinley-Matlock-Derby line instead. With the slopes of Kinder Scout rising steeply from the valley bottom, Class 114 cars E50003 and E56019 head west from Edale with a Sheffield-New Mills Central stopping train on 26 March 1981. *(Paul Shannon)*

Today's stopping trains in the Hope Valley generally work through between Manchester Piccadilly and Sheffield. A pair of Northern Class 150 units headed by 150148 passes Earles Sidings with the 1249 departure from Manchester Piccadilly on 29 September 2020. Newer Class 195 units have since begun to appear on this route. *(Paul Shannon)*

Nine years after the last Manchester-bound express used its now trackless Down platform, Matlock station presents rather a sorry sight as a six-car Class 120 and Class 104 combination stands in the former Up platform on 14 April 1977. The rusty rails in the foreground belong to the run-round loop, which would have seen only occasional use by that time. *(Paul Shannon)*

Class 121 car 55033 was uniquely repainted in the West Midlands 'Midline' livery in 1986, a scheme which it retained until its withdrawal in 1995. It is pictured near Duffield with the 1106 Matlock-Derby service on 30 October 1989. The vehicle was subsequently preserved and has worked on a number of heritage railways. *(Paul Shannon)*

Despite serving a densely populated area – one of the six towns that make up the borough of Stoke-on-Trent – Longton station lost its ticket office in the 1990s. Today the platforms are supervised by security cameras instead. East Midlands Trains (EMT) car 153374 rolls into Longton with the 1542 Derby-Crewe service on 24 March 2016. At that time EMT operated a sizeable fleet of Class 153s, but they were all retired by EMT's successor East Midlands Railway by the end of 2021. *(Paul Shannon)*

The delightful 1884 signal box at Scropton, between Tutbury & Hatton and Uttoxeter, sets the scene for East Midlands Railway (EMR) unit 170532 forming the 1011 Crewe-Newark Castle service on 12 August 2022. EMR received its first Class 170s in March 2020 and they have gradually replaced older units on various secondary routes. *(Paul Shannon)*

boxes survive at Totley Tunnel East, Grindleford, Earles Sidings and Edale.

After the Buxton-Matlock line closed in 1968, Matlock found itself at the end of a branch line from Ambergate. Further economies were made as the intermediate stations lost their staff and in 1969 the line was singled. However, a small revival took place in May 1972 when Matlock Bath reopened as an unstaffed halt, the local Chamber of Trade having contributed to the cost.

A more ambitious project which sadly ended in failure was the reopening of the short branch to Sinfin on the south side of Derby, to be served by extending workings to and from Matlock. Trains began running to Sinfin on 4 October 1976, calling at the reopened Peartree station on the main line as well as two new branch stations at Sinfin North and Sinfin Central. Unfortunately, the trains were not frequent enough to attract lots of passengers and the stations were of limited use – Sinfin North had access to and from adjacent factories only and Sinfin Central was hidden away at the end of a narrow, enclosed footpath. The service was reduced to one train a day in 1992 and withdrawn altogether in the following year, after which any intending passengers were provided with a taxi to save the railway going through costly closure procedures. Permission to close the line – and therefore discontinue the taxi service – was finally granted in 1998.

Nuneaton Abbey Junction is pictured on 9 April 1984, as the 1543 Leicester-Birmingham New Street heads west after intersecting with the West Coast Main Line at Nuneaton station. The hybrid DMU comprises Class 116 motor vehicles M53118 and M53076 and Class 127 trailer M59598. The Nuneaton avoiding line to the right of the signal box closed in 1992. However, as train frequencies increased, the conflicting movements between WCML and Birmingham-Leicester trains became a headache, and the bridge over the WCML was reinstated in 2004 for a new line serving an island platform on the east side of Nuneaton station. *(Paul Shannon)*

Coventry Arena, which was named after its sponsor Ricoh until 2021, gained its own station on the Coventry-Nuneaton line in 2016. Extraordinarily, however, the use of a Class 153 car with only 75 seats led to the station being closed for one hour before and after matches to prevent spectators from overfilling the train. Unit 153365 forms an afternoon Coventry-Nuneaton working on 12 August 2015 as a Class 66 comes into view with a southbound intermodal train. *(Paul Shannon)*

Mixtures of upper and lower quadrant signals were by no means uncommon, especially on lines that had been transferred between BR regions. Stratford-on-Avon was one such example – a Great Western Railway station which later became part of the BR London Midland Region. Class 122 car M55000 arrives at Stratford with the 0905 from Leamington Spa on 27 October 1984. *(Paul Shannon)*

The Stratford-on-Avon to Leamington Spa service became part of the Chiltern Railways franchise, whereas trains between Stratford-on-Avon and Birmingham went to West Midlands Railway. Chiltern unit 165003 rounds the curve into Hatton station with the 1037 Stratford-Leamington Spa train on 29 October 2018. *(Paul Shannon)*

The Beeching axe fell severely on Walsall and by 1965 the town's only passenger service was on the electrified line from Birmingham via Bescot. Even that service faced an uncertain future in the 1970s. Unit 312202 heads for Walsall after calling at Bescot with the 1751 from Birmingham New Street on 3 July 1987. This unit had recently been painted in Network SouthEast colours ahead of its transfer to the Fenchurch Street-Shoeburyness line. *(Paul Shannon)*

Despite linking two cities, the Derby-Stoke line has always been a secondary route. It lost all but three of its intermediate stations in the 1960s, but since then it has seen little change. In 1973, BR operated a roughly hourly all-stations service, with most trains running through between Lincoln and Crewe. The 1985 timetable followed a broadly similar pattern, but with fewer through trains to and from Lincoln. The station at Tutbury & Hatton was reopened in 1989 with new platforms, one on each side of the level crossing. Today's hourly service generally operates between Newark and Crewe. No less than seven mechanical signal boxes remain in use between Derby and Stoke.

While retaining its service on the Derby-Stoke line, Uttoxeter ceased to be a passenger junction in 1965 when BR closed the remaining portion of the Churnet Valley line between Uttoxeter and Leek.

In Leicestershire, passenger services on the Leicester-Burton line ceased in 1964, making Coalville one of the largest towns in the country without a rail link. The whole line remained open for freight and there is a long-standing campaign for its reopening to passengers. Another loss in the 1960s was the Great Central main line, as mentioned above. Meanwhile the Midland Main Line has had some of its intermediate stations restored, with a new Leicester-Loughborough local service calling at Syston, Sileby and Barrow-on-Soar from 1993. The local service was withdrawn in 2005, but the intermediate stations remained open for calls by Leicester-Lincoln trains.

The Leamington Spa-Coventry-Nuneaton line was a secondary route that lost its local passenger services in 1965 but remained open for freight, diversions and special workings. Five miles of double track on the

From its reopening to passengers in 1989 until its electrification in 2019, the line from Walsall to Hednesford, and later Rugeley, was worked by DMUs. A Class 116/127 combination comprising cars 53073, 59598 and 53865 passes Ryecroft Junction on the approach to Walsall with the 1533 from Hednesford on 17 August 1989. The two tracks curving to the right form the freight-only Sutton Park line. (Paul Shannon)

Leamington Spa-Coventry line were singled in 1972, with a passing loop at Kenilworth. InterCity trains returned to the Leamington Spa-Coventry line in 1977, enabling them to serve Coventry instead of Solihull and giving them an easier route into and out of Birmingham New Street. Eventually the InterCity trains were joined by a local service, which prompted the reopening of Kenilworth station. That project was notoriously slow and expensive to complete, taking five years from the approval of funding to completion in 2018 and costing a staggering £11.3 million for a single platform and buildings. Today, Kenilworth has an hourly service between Leamington Spa and Nuneaton via Coventry, while the line also carries an hourly long-distance service between Manchester and Reading or Bournemouth as well as a good number of freight workings, all of which puts a lot of pressure on the single-track sections.

The Coventry-Nuneaton stretch regained its local passenger service in May 1988, with one intermediate station at Bedworth. Initially, through running between Coventry and Hinckley was possible, but the remodelling of Nuneaton station in the early 2000s put a stop to that. Two further intermediate stations at Coventry Arena and Bermuda Park opened in 2016, by which time the line supported an hourly service.

Local lines in and around Birmingham faced some pruning in the 1960s as passenger numbers fell and competition from road transport intensified. The former Great Western Main Line through Snow Hill Tunnel was severed in 1968, leaving two unconnected termini – Moor Street for trains to Leamington Spa and Stratford-on-Avon, and Snow Hill for trains to Wolverhampton Low Level and Langley Green. The Snow Hill services were withdrawn in 1972.

However, a rethink of local transport needs by the West Midlands Passenger Transport Authority led to the reopening of Snow Hill Tunnel, allowing trains from the south to terminate at Snow Hill station instead of Moor Street from October 1987. The building of through platforms at Moor Street enabled them to call there as well.

Class 121 car M55032 has just arrived at Stourbridge Town at 1402 with one of the regular shuttle services from Stourbridge Junction on 21 June 1986. The service was later taken over by Class 153 cars, and since 2009 it has been worked by one of two Class 139 Parry People Movers. A journey time of just three minutes allows one vehicle to maintain a ten-minute interval service. *(David J. Hayes)*

In 1995, Snow Hill became a through station again when the line to Langley Green via Smethwick reopened to passengers. The third and final stage of the Snow Hill revival was the launch of the Midland Metro between Birmingham and Wolverhampton, using much of the former Great Western route.

While the line to Leamington Spa has always been relatively safe, the North Warwickshire line from Birmingham to Stratford-on-Avon via Henley-in-Arden faced possible closure in the 1970s. The section south of Henley-in-Arden was still under threat as late as 1986, the idea being to divert the Birmingham-Stratford service via Solihull and close the intermediate halt at Wootton Wawen. The threat was eventually dropped and today the North Warwickshire line carries an hourly off-peak service between Stratford-on-Avon and Kidderminster. The single-track link to Hatton is used by a two-hourly local service to Leamington Spa and hourly trains to Kidderminster, alternating with those via Henley, as well as one morning train to and from London Marylebone.

Redditch station became the terminus of a five-mile branch from Barnt Green when the Evesham-Redditch line closed to passengers in 1963. It then faced a precarious existence, with just three trains a day to and from Birmingham in the 1973 timetable. Not until 1980 was an hourly service introduced on the cross-city axis to Lichfield. The demand was proven and the frequency of that service was doubled by the end of the decade. Further growth in passenger numbers saw the Redditch branch electrified in 1993 and a new passing loop at Alvechurch created in 2014, providing more flexibility in the timetable.

The various lines converging on Dudley had lost their passenger services by 1964, including the Stourbridge Junction-Bescot/Walsall line which remained open as a

The railway through Worcester Foregate Street was reconfigured as two separate single-track routes in 1973, with new semaphore signals installed in various places. West Midlands Trains units 172341 and 172217 approach Foregate Street with the 1109 from Dorridge on 27 May 2022. Both tracks are well used throughout the day, with Great Western Railway serving destinations such as London Paddington, Bristol and Weymouth, and West Midlands Trains operating services from Hereford to Birmingham and from Foregate Street to Dorridge and Whitlocks End. *(Paul Shannon)*

through route for freight until 1993. A curious survivor is the Stourbridge Town branch which, with a length of 0.8 miles, is the shortest passenger line on the British network. The station was relocated in 1979 to allow the earlier site to be used for a new bus interchange, and a new station building was opened in 1994. Conventional heavy rail units gave way to Parry People Movers on the branch shuttle in 2009.

Walsall also lost most of its local rail connections in the 1960s, with just the electric service from Birmingham remaining by 1966. The Walsall-Wolverhampton line regained a passenger service in 1998, but funding was later withdrawn and the service finished in 2008. The section between Darlaston and Wolverhampton was used for a time by Wrexham & Shropshire trains to and from Marylebone, and then again in 2022 by West Midlands Trains services between Crewe and Birmingham. The planned reopening of Willenhall and Darlaston stations has been delayed.

A more clear-cut success story is the reopening of the Walsall-Rugeley line. Like most passenger revivals, the line had remained in place for freight. It was also used for excursions and diversions. The reopening as a local passenger route took place in stages: from Walsall to Hednesford in 1989; to Rugeley Town in 1997; and to Rugeley Trent Valley in 1998. The whole line was electrified in 2019, which meant that the diesel service from Walsall could be replaced by through electric trains between Birmingham and Rugeley. A half-hourly frequency is maintained on the route today.

The physical barrier of the Malvern Hills forms an imposing backdrop as a three-car Class 101 unit passes Malvern Wells with the 1605 Hereford-Birmingham New Street on 8 August 1982. The train has just passed through the 1,589-yard Colwall Tunnel, which has always been a single-track pinch point on the Hereford line. Malvern Wells box remains in use today to control the end of the single-track section. *(Paul Shannon)*

The Welsh Marches Line, also known as the North and West Route, declined in importance in the 1960s and became a low priority for investment. Even today, no less than fifteen manual signal boxes remain in use on the 90-mile stretch between Newport and Shrewsbury. Arriva Trains Wales unit 150231 passes Moreton-on-Lugg with the 1330 from Manchester Piccadilly to Swansea on 12 July 2020. *(Paul Shannon)*

Far from their original home territory, Class 33s took over the haulage of some Marches Line trains in 1981. Shrewsbury Abbey forms the backdrop to this view of 33063 approaching Sutton Bridge Junction with the 1602 Crewe-Cardiff train on 10 August 1982. The hauled stock later gave way to various second-generation DMU types including Classes 158 and 175. *(Paul Shannon)*

Wem station was targeted for closure in the Beeching Report, but it survived to be served by local trains between Crewe and Shrewsbury. Class 101 cars M56333 and M51175 form the 1723 Crewe-Shrewsbury stopper on 10 August 1982. The co-acting signal at the end of the northbound platform was soon to be replaced by a colour light, and Wem box closed in October 2013 when the line came under the control of Cardiff Regional Operating Centre. *(Paul Shannon)*

In Worcestershire, the Bromyard branch closed to passengers in 1964. The Worcester-Hereford line remained in use for a mixture of long-distance and local trains, but seven of its intermediate stations closed in 1965 and the stretch between Ledbury and Colwall was singled in 1967. The route through Worcester Foregate Street was re-signalled and remodelled in 1973, with two independent single lines from Henwick leading to Worcester Shrub Hill and Droitwich Spa respectively. At the Hereford end of the line, the stretch between Ledbury and Shelwick was singled and re-signalled in 1984. Little change has taken place since then and Worcester is still a hot spot for semaphore signals. Manual boxes survive at Worcester Tunnel Junction, Worcester Shrub Hill, Henwick, Newland, Malvern Wells and Ledbury.

The Severn Valley Line from Bewdley to Shrewsbury closed in 1963, paving the way for the formation of the Severn Valley Railway Society two years later and the eventual reopening as a heritage operation to Bridgnorth. The two routes to Bewdley from Hartlebury and Kidderminster survived a few years longer; in 1969 BR ran a sparse service on those routes including peak-hour trains from Bewdley to Birmingham and back and a few through workings between Hartlebury and Kidderminster reversing at Bewdley. However, the service was withdrawn in January 1970 and both Bewdley and Stourport stations closed. Once freight traffic to Foley Park sugar factory between Kidderminster and Bewdley had finished in 1982, the Severn Valley Railway was able to extend its operation to Kidderminster.

The Shropshire town of Wellington, now effectively part of Telford, fared badly in the 1960s with the loss of three of its five railway routes – to Much Wenlock, Nantwich and Stafford – as well as the withdrawal of

The Shrewsbury-Chester line lost its status as an express route when the last Paddington-Birkenhead trains were withdrawn in 1967. Gobowen station retained a generous track layout, with sidings on both sides of the line and the Oswestry branch diverging to the right, when Class 101 cars M51179 and M56358 were photographed forming the 1150 Wolverhampton-Chester service on 11 August 1982. *(Paul Shannon)*

local services to Shrewsbury. Local trains continued to run on the Wolverhampton-Wellington-Shrewsbury axis, but one further loss was the closure of New Hadley halt between Wellington and Oakengates in 1985. However, in the following year BR opened the new station at Telford Central, just east of Oakengates. It was intended to cater for InterCity traffic to and from London, but these days the emphasis is more on local and middle-distance journeys.

The Shrewsbury-Crewe line was expected to lose all its intermediate stations except Whitchurch in the 1960s, but in fact they survived. In 1969 BR served the line with eight stopping trains each way on weekdays; that figure had increased by the mid-1980s, although not all local trains stopped at all stations. Today the smaller stations such as Yorton have a roughly two-hourly service throughout the day, whereas Nantwich and Whitchurch are served by some long-distance trains between Manchester or Crewe and South Wales as well as by the local workings. Less fortunate was the former Cambrian branch from Whitchurch to Oswestry and Welshpool; its passenger service was withdrawn in 1965 and the line abandoned.

In the Potteries district, local passenger services on the short branch to Silverdale and on the loop line to Kidsgrove via Burslem ceased in 1964. The main line through Stoke-on-Trent continued to carry a mixture of long-distance and local trains after electrification was completed in 1967. The off-peak local service in 1985 consisted of roughly hourly stopping trains from Manchester to Stoke-on-Trent, with every other train continuing south to Stafford. However, this all changed in 2004, when Central Trains withdrew from the Stoke-Stafford route, leaving no service at Wedgwood, Barlaston, Stone and Norton Bridge. The service to Stone was restored in 2008, initially with hourly trains between Crewe and London Euston. They now run between Crewe and Birmingham. The other stations south of Stoke were less fortunate: Norton Bridge was officially closed in 2017, while Wedgwood and Barlaston are still officially open but served only by replacement buses.

CHAPTER 5

WALES

The outlook for the Welsh railway network in the 1960s was bleak. Most of the cross-country routes were under threat of closure, as were some local lines in the South Wales valleys. The direct links between North Wales and Mid-Wales, and between Mid-Wales and South Wales, faced the axe, so that any through traffic on the north-south axis would have to use the Marches Line via Shrewsbury.

The dense network of lines radiating north from Newport and Cardiff was focused primarily on coal. Of those lines that also carried a local passenger service, only the branches to Barry, Rhymney, Merthyr Tydfil and Treherbert were expected to survive into the 1970s. By and large, that is exactly what happened. Between 1962 and 1964 BR withdrew passenger services from the Ebbw Vale and Abertillery/Nantyglo branches, the Pontypool-Aberdare-Neath line, the Barry-Pontypridd line, both Aberdare branches (Vale of Neath and Taff Vale), the Maerdy branch and the Vale of Glamorgan line between Barry and Bridgend. The Penarth-Cadoxton

The Great Western lamp hut adds a delightful touch to this wintry scene at Heath Junction, as a Class 116 unit heads south with a train from Rhymney to Penarth in 1978. The Coryton branch diverges to the left. Heath Junction signal box looks somewhat forlorn; it closed in 1984 in favour of a portable cabin. *(Michael Rhodes)*

Two Class 116 units cross at Walnut Tree Junction on the morning of 14 April 1982, with Taffs Well station visible in the background. The tracks curving to the right form the freight-only spur to Aber, which was taken out of regular use in June 1982. Walnut Tree Junction box closed in January 1997, just before the Radyr area re-signalling. *(Paul Shannon)*

Pontypridd station was reduced to a single platform face in 1974, which created a bottleneck for trains on the Treherbert and Merthyr lines. Class 116 cars W50128, W59036 and W50086 call at Pontypridd with a Cardiff-bound working on 14 April 1982. A new northbound platform was provided in 1990/91 and a south-facing bay was added in 2014, providing much-needed extra capacity as traffic in the valleys grew. *(Paul Shannon)*

line closed in 1968, while the Bridgend-Tondu-Maesteg-Treherbert line closed in two stages: the section between Cymmer Afan and Treherbert was taken out of use in February 1968 due to the poor state of the 3,443-yard Rhondda Tunnel – the third longest railway tunnel in Wales – and the rest of the line lost its regular service in June 1970. A further small closure was the branch extension from Barry Island to Barry Pier, with an official date of July 1976 although trains had actually ceased in October 1971.

The early 1970s was a low point for the passenger network in the Valleys, as even the surviving lines were rationalised to reduce costs. By 1975 the branches were all singled at their extremities: the Barry Island branch from Barry; the Penarth branch from Cogan Junction; the Rhymney branch from Bargoed; the Merthyr branch from Abercynon; and the Treherbert branch from Cwmparc.

The 1980s then saw the beginnings of a revival. The fact that so many branches remained in place for coal traffic meant that their reopening to passengers was possible. But the window of opportunity was short as the pits closed one after the other. By way of a modest start, BR restored local passenger services in October 1987 on the City Line between Cardiff Central and Radyr via Ninian Park, to be served mostly by through trains to and from Coryton. This through running made good operational sense because it reduced the number of trains terminating or starting at Cardiff Central.

The first passenger revival in the Valleys proper was the Aberdare branch, with services resuming in October 1988. Trains used the 1973 connection at Cwmbach so that they ran over former Taff Vale metals from Abercynon to Cwmbach and then over the former Vale of Neath line from Cwmbach to Aberdare. Stations were provided

The Treherbert branch was singled beyond Ystrad Rhondda in 1972 and between Porth and Ystrad Rhondda in 1981, leaving a passing loop at Ystrad Rhondda. Class 116 cars W51139, W59033 and W51152 amble down the valley near Treorchy with the 1232 Treherbert-Barry Island train on 15 April 1982. *(Paul Shannon)*

at Abercynon North, where the track layout precluded calling at the existing Abercynon station, Penrhiwceiber, Mountain Ash, Fernhill and Cwmbach. Passenger numbers grew beyond expectations and in the early 2000s the line benefited from longer station platforms as well as a passing loop at Mountain Ash. The original Abercynon station was rebuilt in 2008 to allow Aberdare trains to call there and Abercynon North closed.

The second South Wales reopening saw the Bridgend-Maesteg branch return to the passenger map in October 1992. Intermediate stations were opened at Wildmill, Sarn, Tondu, Garth and Maesteg Ewenny Road. All were newly built structures except for Tondu, where the pre-1970 platform was still usable. Since the Maesteg trains used the South Wales Main Line between Bridgend and Cardiff, the opportunity was taken to reopen two stations on that stretch, at Pontyclun and Pencoed. A third station, Llanharan, followed in 2007.

The Vale of Glamorgan line from Barry to Bridgend regained a regular passenger service in June 2005, with intermediate stations at Llantwit Major and Rhoose. In this instance the track had been maintained to passenger standards since the withdrawal of the previous local service, mainly for use by diversions when the South Wales Main Line was undergoing maintenance.

The Ebbw Vale branch, once busy with steel as well as coal traffic, lay in a state of limbo for several years before its reopening to passengers in February 2008. Stations were provided at Rogerstone, Risca & Pontymister, Crosskeys, Newbridge, Llanhilleth and Ebbw Vale Parkway. Trains used the south-facing curve at Park Junction to run to and from Cardiff. A further intermediate station at Pye Corner opened in 2014 and the branch was extended to Ebbw Vale Town in 2015. The north-facing curve at Park Junction came back into use in December 2021 when the Ebbw Vale-Cardiff trains were joined by a Crosskeys-Newport service.

Today's timetable in the Valleys provides an off-peak service of two trains an hour on most routes, but only one train an hour from Crosskeys to Ebbw Vale, from Bargoed to Rhymney and on the Vale of Glamorgan line. Penarth and Barry Island enjoy four and three trains an hour respectively. Fifty years ago, trains in the Valleys were much less frequent, with most of the routes having an hourly off-peak service.

The Beeching Report foresaw the closure of all remaining routes heading north from Neath, Swansea and Carmarthen. The Neath & Brecon Line closed to passengers in 1962 and the Vale of Neath Line to Hirwaun succumbed in 1964. The lines from Carmarthen to Aberystwyth and Llandeilo lost their passenger services between 1963 and 1965. The Cardigan branch closed to passengers in 1962.

The unexpected survivor, however, was the 90-mile, largely single-track, Central Wales Line from Llanelli to Craven Arms, complete with its 27 intermediate stations and halts. Consent for closure was given only for the direct link between Pontarddulais and Swansea Victoria, which duly carried its last passenger trains in 1964. Through trains between Swansea and Craven Arms then needed to reverse at Llanelli. From the mid-1960s the train frequency on the Central Wales Line remained fairly constant, with timetables showing four trains each way in 1967, five in 1972 and five in 1985. The track was rationalised wherever possible and by the mid-1970s the line had the longest block section on BR, comprising 31 miles of single track from Llandrindod to Craven Arms.

The signalling on the Central Wales Line was modernised in 1986, when No-Signalman Token Remote (NSTR) operation allowed the closure of the intermediate signal boxes at Llandeilo, Llandovery, Llanwrtyd and Llandrindod. The system was supervised from Pantyffynnon box. Unlike the Radio Electric Token Block (RETB) system used on some rural lines, NSTR did not

BR Sprinter unit 150261 passes the distinctively elevated Ystrad Mynach South box with a Rhymney to Merthyr service in 1992. This working used the Ninian Park line so that it could run through Cardiff without reversing. Ystrad Mynach South box closed in 2013 when Cardiff Regional Operating Centre took control of the Rhymney branch. *(Michael Rhodes)*

The Rhymney branch became well known for its use of Class 37s in the early 2000s. Making a change from the usual 37/4 sub-class, retro rail blue-liveried 37023 calls at Bargoed with the 0740 Rhymney-Cardiff on 27 July 2000. This spell of locomotive haulage ended in December 2005, but Class 37s plied the Rhymney branch once again in 2019/20 to cover a unit shortage. *(Michael Rhodes)*

Once a bustling freight location with the frequent clanking of loose-coupled coal wagons, Tondu regained its passenger service when the Maesteg branch reopened in 1992. By that time all the pits in the area had closed and the line from Tondu to Margam was rarely used. Sprinter unit 150282 passes the 1884 Tondu Middle box with the 0800 Maesteg-Cheltenham train on 18 August 2009. *(Paul Shannon)*

require trains to carry any special equipment. The long section between Llandrindod and Craven Arms was broken by the reinstatement of Knighton loop in 1990.

The number of intermediate stations between Llanelli and Craven Arms rose to twenty-eight in 1984 when the tiny Sugar Loaf halt was reopened between Llanwrtyd and Cynghordy. Located near the summit of the line and some distance from the nearest road, Sugar Loaf has often ranked among the least-used stations in Britain – although the publication of that fact prompted a rise in usage to 1,846 passengers in 2017/18.

Today the Central Wales Line carries a weekday service of four trains each way over its whole length, plus two trains that cover only part of the line – an early morning working from Carmarthen to Llandovery which returns to Swansea and another morning working from Shrewsbury to Llandrindod and back to Crewe.

In West Wales, the short branch from Johnston to Neyland closed in 1964, but the other lines to the Pembrokeshire coast all survived. The 27-mile Pembroke Dock branch has always been busy with holiday traffic, especially to and from the Tenby area. However, economies have been made. The last crossing point on the line, at Tenby station, lost its signal box in 1988 in favour of NSTR operation controlled from Whitland. The run-round loop at Pembroke Dock was taken out of use in 2016. The frequency of local trains has increased in recent decades, with Transport for Wales now offering roughly one train every two hours.

Milford Haven is the busiest of the three branch termini in Pembrokeshire. Intermediate signal boxes at Johnston and Haverfordwest were closed in 1988 and the line is now controlled from Clarbeston Road. In 1972 there were seven weekday departures from Milford Haven,

Transport for Wales became the last operator of Class 142 and Class 143 Pacer units on the British main line, with its final Class 143 vehicles retiring from service in May 2021. Unit 142074 leads a four-car formation away from Barry Docks on 20 July 2020. This was during the height of the coronavirus pandemic, when passengers were few but trains were long to enable social distancing. *(Paul Shannon)*

including one train with day coaches and another with sleeping cars for Paddington. Today's timetable shows ten weekday departures, of which six are through trains to Manchester Piccadilly via the Marches Line.

The line to Fishguard Harbour has long been dominated by maritime traffic, especially after the withdrawal of all services from Fishguard & Goodwick except Motorail trains in 1964. The timetable for 1972 shows just two weekday departures from Fishguard Harbour, plus a third service operating only on certain days of the week. The last two signal boxes on the line, at Fishguard & Goodwick and Letterston, closed in 1983 and 1987 respectively. However, a small revival took place in May 2012, when Fishguard & Goodwick station reopened in conjunction with an increased train frequency. Today's timetable shows six weekday departures, of which two are through workings to Cardiff.

The Cambrian Lines from Shrewsbury to Aberystwyth and Pwllheli were largely spared by the Beeching Report, other than a recommendation to close some of the intermediate stations between Shrewsbury and Aberystwyth, which went ahead as planned. However the line heading north from Buttington to Oswestry and Whitchurch lost its passenger service completely in 1965, as did the Llanfyllin branch. The Barmouth-Dolgellau branch was another 1965 closure, along with its former Great Western continuation from Dolgellau to Bala, Llangollen and Ruabon.

While the line from Shrewsbury to Aberystwyth was regarded as safe, the 53-mile coastal route from Dovey Junction to Pwllheli with its twenty-eight intermediate stations and halts was a different matter. A formal proposal for its closure was made in October 1971. Opposition was considerable and the Cambrian Coast Line Action Group even ran a special train from Pwllheli to Euston in November 1972 to present a petition to Downing Street. The line gained its reprieve in 1974.

Even after that, there were challenges. The discovery of a marine woodworm attack on Barmouth Bridge in 1980 led to fears that the line beyond Tywyn might close. In the event, repairs were authorised and completed in 1985/86. Another threat arose in 2018 due to the poor condition of the bridge; however, a £3 million restoration project was started in 2020 and ought to ensure the line's survival.

Rationalisation on the Cambrian lines included the removal of Borth passing loop in 1973, creating a long single-track section from Dovey Junction to Aberystwyth. On the coastal line, Pwllheli signal box was reduced to a shunting frame in 1976 and Criccieth lost its passing loop and box in 1977. This resulted in one train working between Porthmadog and Pwllheli, although trains could still be shut in at Pwllheli. Black Rock halt had become decrepit and almost inaccessible

Transport for Wales inherited a fleet of Class 170 Turbostar units from Greater Anglia and used them on the Ebbw Vale and Maesteg routes among others. 170206 passes the fine array of lower quadrants at Park Junction while working the 0842 Ebbw Vale-Cardiff Central service on 16 June 2021. At that time the direct service to Newport had not yet started. *(Paul Shannon)*

Converted from Class 319 EMUs, nine Class 769 bi-mode units entered service with Transport for Wales in 2020/21. Their commissioning had been much delayed because of technical issues and the suspension of training during the pandemic. Unit 769007 enters the single-track section as it recedes from Bargoed with the 0916 from Cardiff Central to Rhymney on 15 June 2022. *(Paul Shannon)*

Showing the headlight which was a requirement on the Central Wales Line, Class 101 cars W51449 and W51521 pull into Llandovery station with the 1050 Shrewsbury-Swansea train on 5 July 1985. The combination of two power cars was useful for the gradients of up to 1 in 60 on this route. The box and signals would be taken out of use in the following year. *(Paul Shannon)*

Southern Region Class 33s began reaching West Wales on regular passenger diagrams in 1982. They worked to both Milford Haven and Fishguard. 33005 is about to run round its rake of Mark 1 stock at Milford Haven after forming the 1402 service from Swansea on 10 July 1984. The former station buildings had been demolished a few years earlier. *(Paul Shannon)*

Having drawn its custom from a morning sailing from Rosslare, 47492 sets out from Fishguard Harbour with the 1310 to London Paddington on 10 July 1984. The through Paddington trains later switched to InterCity 125 stock and were withdrawn altogether in 2003, having only run overnight in the last few years. *(Paul Shannon)*

In 1990 the Pembroke Dock branch was still served by locomotive-hauled holiday trains to Tenby as well as by InterCity 125 workings. With the NSTR signs standing prominently at the end of both platforms, InterCity-liveried 47817 arrives at Tenby with a short rake of mainly Mark 2 air-conditioned stock forming the 0752 from Leeds. *(Paul Shannon)*

by the mid-1970s and trains stopped calling there in 1976. Gogarth and Abertafol halts were also in poor condition but remained in use until 1984, their official closure taking place in the following year. Llangelynin halt closed in 1991 because the expense of repairing the platform and installing lighting could not be justified.

The introduction of RETB signalling on the Cambrian network in 1988 was a significant step. Signal boxes at Welshpool, Newtown, Talerddig, Dovey Junction, Tywyn, Barmouth South, Harlech and Porthmadog were all closed, with the new system controlled from Machynlleth. Further change came with the replacement of RETB by the European Rail Traffic Management System (ERTMS) in 2010/11. The main visual change with ERTMS is the removal of all lineside signalling equipment. In addition, a passing loop was restored on the Aberystwyth line at Dovey Junction.

The 1972 timetable on the Cambrian lines included six weekday departures from Pwllheli, one from Barmouth and eight from Aberystwyth. On Summer Saturdays a loco-hauled train ran from Aberystwyth to London Euston. Fifty years later, Transport for Wales offers a much-improved local service with eight weekday departures from Pwllheli, one from Barmouth and sixteen from Aberystwyth. The Aberystwyth branch has also benefited from the reopening of Bow Street station in 2021. However, the through London train is a distant memory.

In North Wales, the line from Wrexham to Ellesmere closed in 1962 and the former Great Central lines from Wrexham to Chester Northgate and Bidston were also under threat. While the Chester Northgate branch closed in 1968, the Wrexham-Bidston service survived. Facilities at the Wrexham Central terminus were scaled

Long DMU formations were not uncommon in the 1970s, especially on weekend holiday trains. A nine-car train led by two three-car Class 101 sets departs from Barmouth with the 1730 to Birmingham New Street on 3 August 1975. On the left is the former excursion platform which had also been used by Dolgellau trains until 1965. On the right is Barmouth South signal box, which closed as a block post in 1988 but remained in situ until 1999 when it was moved to the Llangollen Railway. *(David Rapson)*

Park Royal Class 103 DMUs were a familiar sight on the Cambrian Coast in the 1970s. They were based at Chester depot and also had duties along the North Wales Coast. Cars M56164 and M50398 arrive at Harlech with a Pwllheli-Birmingham train on 26 September 1978, as 25325 waits for its northbound path with the pick-up goods train to Pwllheli. The Class 103s were a target for early withdrawal and the last vehicle was retired in 1983. *(Paul Shannon)*

With an eye-watering price tag of £8 million, the unstaffed platform at Bow Street opened on 14 February 2021, some 56 years after the original station in the village had been axed. It was the first station to open in Wales since Pye Corner in December 2014 and would be served by all trains to and from Aberystwyth. Transport for Wales unit 158821 arrives at Bow Street with the 1128 Aberystwyth-Birmingham International on 29 April 2022. *(Paul Shannon)*

A fleet of Class 120 cross-country units was based at Chester from the late 1970s and worked on the Chester-Shrewsbury line as well as on former Cambrian metals to Aberystwyth. Cars M50668, M59262 and M50721 pass Croes Newydd North Fork signal box as they set out from Wrexham with the 1523 from Chester to Wolverhampton on 11 August 1982. The box is still in use today, but the semaphores are long gone. *(Paul Shannon)*

In 1973 Wrexham Central was reduced to a single platform station with minimal facilities. But at least it survived, unlike many other secondary lines that were earmarked for closure in the 1960s. Class 108 cars M50925 and M51565 await departure from Wrexham Central with the 1625 to Bidston on 11 August 1982. The platform was relocated a short distance further west in 1998 to permit redevelopment of the original site. *(Paul Shannon)*

Having just crossed the invisible border from England into Wales, Class 108 cars M51563 and M50926 pass Shotwick with the 1528 from Birkenhead North to Wrexham Central on 11 May 1977. Once the iron ore trains from Birkenhead to Shotton had finished, BR could lengthen the block sections on the line and Shotwick Sidings box closed in June 1982. *(David Rapson)*

Transport for Wales received five Vivarail Class 230 diesel-battery hybrid units in 2020 with the intention of phasing them into revenue-earning service on the Wrexham-Bidston line. Unfortunately, the plan was delayed by various problems including 'thermal issues', a euphemism for one of the units catching fire near Wrexham. Unit 230006 passes Penyffordd with the 0940 Wrexham Central-Bidston test run on 1 September 2020. *(Paul Shannon)*

A four-car DMU with a Class 103 set at the rear departs from Llandudno with a local train for Llandudno Junction and beyond on 12 June 1977. A Class 47 awaits departure with a long-distance train on the left. The signalman has apparently driven his Ford Anglia Estate down the station platform and parked it between the tracks, something which would have been entirely normal in those days. *(Paul Shannon)*

back with the withdrawal of station staff in 1972 and the reduction to a single-track stub in the following year. The station would be relocated 400 yards to the west in 1998 to allow redevelopment of the original site. At the northern end of the line, trains terminated at Birkenhead North on weekdays and New Brighton on Sundays from 1971 until 1978, when they were amended to reverse at Bidston. The service frequency has changed little in the past 50 years.

Along the North Wales Coast, the Beeching Report recommended the closure of some smaller stations on the main line, as well as total closure of the branches to Blaenau Ffestiniog, Caernarfon/Afon Wen and Amlwch. The closure of the small stations on the main line went ahead in 1966, although four of them have since reopened – Shotton Low Level in 1972, Llanfairpwll in 1973, Valley in 1982 and Conwy in 1987. The Amlwch branch lost its passenger service in 1964, although it remained open for freight until 1993. The line from Bangor to Afon Wen was cut back to Caernarfon in 1964 and closed completely to passenger traffic in 1970, with just an emergency Freightliner service operating to Caernarfon until 1972 while the Britannia Bridge was being rebuilt after a fire.

The Conwy Valley Line from Llandudno Junction to Blaenau Ffestiniog survived the closure threat, partly thanks to the important nuclear traffic from Trawsfynydd that used the line. The intermediate station at Glan Conwy closed in 1964 but reopened as an unstaffed halt in 1970, by which time Paytrain operation on the branch was well established. The former London & North Western terminus at Blaenau Ffestiniog North was replaced in 1982 by a new interchange with the extended Ffestiniog Railway at Blaenau Ffestiniog Central. The village of Llanrwst gained a second station in 1989, more conveniently

Re-signalling along the North Wales Coast has been a long, slow process. Today the semaphores still linger on the Llandudno and Blaenau Ffestiniog branches as well as on the main line on the Isle of Anglesey. Transport for Wales unit 175008 rolls into Deganwy station with the 1141 from Llandudno to Manchester Airport on 18 March 2022. *(Paul Shannon)*

The unkempt platform and disused station building are characteristic of the era as Class 101 cars M56333, M51185, M56334 and M51197 call at Llanrwst with the 1545 from Llandudno Junction to Blaenau Ffestiniog on 29 June 1976. The station building was Grade II listed in 1993 and the passing loop remains in use today, but passenger numbers have declined since the opening of the new Llanrwst station closer to the village centre in 1989. This original station is now named North Llanrwst. *(David Rapson)*

It was not until 1982 that Conwy Valley passenger trains were extended to a new Blaenau Ffestiniog terminus roughly on the site of the former GWR station, also accommodating the newly extended Ffestiniog Railway. Single car 153327 waits at the standard-gauge platform on 16 September 2006 after forming the 1314 from Llandudno, while a Ffestiniog Railway Fairlie tank has just arrived from Porthmadog. *(Paul Shannon)*

located than the original facility which was renamed North Llanrwst. Unfortunately, the Conwy Valley Line is prone to flooding and services have been suspended on more than one occasion while repairs are carried out; nevertheless, this meandering and highly scenic route seems reasonably secure.

CHAPTER 6

NORTH WEST ENGLAND

This area covers both the busy urban routes radiating from Liverpool and Manchester as well as a good number of rural lines. The Beeching Report targeted both types of railway. Duplicate lines were especially vulnerable, but even some large population centres would have had their rail connection axed if the recommendations of the Report had been implemented in full.

On the Wirral, the electrified branches to New Brighton, West Kirby and Rock Ferry were seen as safe in the 1960s and benefited from the opening of the Liverpool loop serving Moorfields, Lime Street and Central Low Level in October 1977. Rock Ferry became an end-on junction in 1969 when Birkenhead Woodside closed and diesel trains from Chester terminated at Rock Ferry instead. The third rail was extended from Rock Ferry to Hooton in 1985 and then from Hooton to Chester in 1993 and Ellesmere Port in 1994.

The line to Ellesmere Port had once been earmarked for closure and its electrification was a welcome

The island platform at Bidston became the interchange point between the Wirral electrics and trains to and from Wrexham in 1978. Two examples of ageing rolling stock are pictured at Bidston on 17 February 2022: Merseyrail unit 507023 calls with the 0916 service from West Kirby to Liverpool (and back to West Kirby), while Transport for Wales unit 150251 is about to depart with the 0932 to Wrexham Central. *(Paul Shannon)*

In the days when BR ran a diesel service between Hooton and Helsby, Gloucester Class 100 cars M56105 and M50350 call at Little Sutton with the 1132 from Hooton to Helsby on 10 July 1979. The line between Hooton and Ellesmere Port is now part of the electrified Merseyrail network and gained an additional station at Overpool in 1988. *(David Rapson)*

turnaround. However, it left the onward route from Ellesmere Port to Helsby in a precarious position, requiring its own diesel service for very low passenger numbers. By 1996 a token service of two trains a day each way was being offered between Ellesmere Port and Helsby, and that frequency is maintained today with one train in the early morning and the other in the evening. The intermediate station at Stanlow was taken out of use – but not officially closed – in February 2022 because of concerns over the safety of its footbridge.

Heading east from Chester, the line to Crewe has always been an important long-distance route, but it lost its local service with closure of Waverton in 1965 and Tattenhall Road and Beeston Castle & Tarporley in 1966. The only change on the Mid-Cheshire line to Northwich was the closure of Chester Northgate station in 1969, with trains diverted over a new connection at Mickle Trafford into Chester General instead. On the former joint line to Warrington, again the plan was to axe local services and close the intermediate stations.

However, that did not happen and both Helsby and Frodsham are very much alive today. The regular local service between Chester and Liverpool via the Halton Curve was withdrawn in 1975, but the track remained in place, albeit latterly only in the northbound direction, and hourly trains recommenced in May 2019.

Local routes to the south and west of Manchester looked set for severe pruning in the 1960s. Early casualties included the services from Glazebrook to Wigan Central and from Glazebrook to Stockport Tiviot Dale in 1964. A small part of the latter route returned to use by passenger trains when the Altrincham-Manchester direct line was converted to Metrolink and the BR service was diverted via Northenden in 1992.

The last passenger trains to serve Tiviot Dale were those on the Manchester Central-Chinley-Sheffield route and they were withdrawn in 1967. That closure left Manchester Central with only two local services, to Chester and Liverpool, and the diversion of those services into Manchester Oxford Road enabled the complete

The nameless signal box at Delamere greets a six-car Class 108 DMU led by Class 108 cars M50940 and M56223 on 20 April 1976. The working is the 1228 from Chester to Manchester Oxford Road, which at that time still took the direct line from Altrincham to Manchester via Sale. Delamere box closed in the following month, its function being replaced by intermediate block signals. *(David Rapson)*

closure of Central in May 1969. Beyond Romiley, the branches to Hayfield and to Macclesfield via Rose Hill were both threatened with closure. Services to Hayfield and on the Rose Hill-Macclesfield stretch ceased in January 1970, but Rose Hill was a busy commuter station and became the terminus of a short branch from Marple Wharf Junction.

The local electric service from Manchester to Glossop and Hadfield survived despite its inclusion in the Beeching list. Conversely, the through service to Sheffield via Hadfield and Woodhead was expected to survive but ceased in January 1970. The Glossop/Hadfield line passed through some densely populated areas and gained some new intermediate stations – Hattersley in 1978, Flowery Field in 1985 and Godley in 1986. The new Godley station led to the closure of the poorly situated original station at Godley Junction in 1995.

The whole of the ex-LNWR Stockport-Buxton line was earmarked for closure in the Beeching Report, as was the former Midland Railway spur from Miller's Dale to Buxton. The latter route closed in 1967, but Buxton retained its connection to Stockport and Manchester. The section between Stockport and Hazel Grove was electrified in 1981 and that section also now carries long-distance trains on the Manchester-Sheffield axis since the opening of the Hazel Grove chord in 1986.

Two further routes on the east side of Manchester survived the threat of closure in the 1960s. One was the link from Hyde Junction to Romiley and the other was the local service between Stockport and Stalybridge via Guide Bridge. However, one reason for keeping the Stockport-Stalybridge service was to provide a connection between Euston-Manchester Piccadilly trains and those on the Trans-Pennine route via Manchester Victoria. Once the Trans-Pennine trains were rerouted via Piccadilly, the Stockport-Stalybridge service was reduced to just one train a week, and that is how it remains today.

North of Manchester, the Beeching Report targeted the electrified line from Victoria to Bury and its diesel-worked extensions to Bacup and Accrington. The Stubbins-Accrington and Rawtenstall-Bacup sections closed in 1966, while the Bury-Rawtenstall service continued until 1972. The fact that the Rawtenstall line remained open for freight until 1980 made it possible for the East Lancashire Railway to take over the route and turn it into a thriving heritage operation. The Manchester-Bury line was converted to Metrolink operation in 1992.

The east-west line from Rochdale to Bolton via Bury Knowsley Street was initially not on the withdrawal list but closed to passengers in October 1970. The Oldham-Rochdale line was similarly spared in the 1960s list but very nearly closed in 1972 and only survived because the South East Lancashire and North East Cheshire (later Greater Manchester) Passenger Transport Executive agreed to support it. The section from Shaw & Crompton to Rochdale was singled in 1980 and the whole loop from Manchester to Rochdale via Oldham was converted to Metrolink operation in 2009/10.

The short branch from Blackrod to Horwich closed to passengers in 1965 and the Leigh loop with its four intermediate stations closed in May 1969. The Manchester-Walkden-Wigan line lost its expresses, but its local service improved from irregular intervals with long gaps in the early 1970s to five trains every two hours in the off-peak today. The Bolton-Wigan line also has a much-improved local service compared with the early 1970s.

Plumley West is the last island of semaphore signalling on the Mid-Cheshire line between Chester and Altrincham. The box was located here to control access to the nearby Ammonia Soda Company works, long since abandoned. Units 150118 and 150132 pass Plumley West with the 0802 from Chester to Manchester Piccadilly on 8 April 2022. *(Paul Shannon)*

Guide Bridge was once a busy four-platform station, where the Stockport-Stalybridge line intersected with the electrified Woodhead route and the diesel branch to Romiley. Class 100 cars M56113 and M50358 cross over onto the main line with a Stalybridge-Stockport service on 9 January 1979. The sidings behind Ashton Junction box hold a typical selection of classes 76 and 40. The box was renamed Guide Bridge in December 1984 and it closed completely in December 2011, when control passed to Manchester East Signalling Control Centre. *(Paul Shannon)*

Located in Derbyshire but within easy commuting range of Manchester, Glossop was served by the small fleet of unique 1,500V DC Class 506 EMUs from the 1950s until the line was converted to standard 25kV AC in 1984. Vehicle M59404M leads a three-car class 506 formation at Glossop on the evening of 8 July 1983, the stock having recently been repainted blue and grey. The short branch from Dinting to Glossop had been singled in 1968. *(Paul Shannon)*

The 22-lever signal box at Furness Vale has outlived most others on the Buxton branch because it controls a level crossing which would be difficult to automate. A five-car DMU slows on the approach to Furness Vale with a Buxton train on 17 August 1988. The first three vehicles are Class 108 cars 52090, 59149 and 51945, while at the rear are Class 127 cars 55978 and 55968 which had been converted to carry parcels. *(Paul Shannon)*

Reddish South has a dedicated group of supporters who would love to see their station's service increase from one train a week to something more useful. In the meantime, the line through Reddish South is used mainly by freight and empty stock workings. Unit 150124 passes through with the 1125 Stockport-Newton Heath empty stock movement on 26 August 2021. *(Paul Shannon)*

In contrast to its two neighbours, suburban Bromley Cross and post-industrial Darwen, Entwistle station serves a sparsely populated rural area. Entwistle lost its station staff in 1971 and its buildings in the following year; the line between Bromley Cross and Darwen was then singled in 1973. Class 105 power cars M50453 and M50520 call at Entwistle with a train for Blackburn on 30 June 1982. *(Paul Shannon)*

The Class 504 units were the second generation of electric stock used on the Manchester Victoria-Bury line, which was first electrified in 1916 with a unique system of side-contact current collection. The Class 504s worked the line from 1959 until the line closed for conversion to Metrolink in 1991. Cars M65450 and M77171 pause at Heaton Park with the 1450 Manchester-Bury train on 16 May 1977. (David Rapson)

On Merseyside, today's network looks rather healthier than it would have done if the planned 1960s closures had gone ahead. On the south side of the city, Liverpool Central High Level lost its Manchester trains when they were diverted to Lime Street in 1966, leaving just the Gateacre service which eked out a precarious existence until April 1972. By the end, Liverpool Central High Level had shrunk from a six-platform main-line terminus to a single short platform, surrounded by dereliction and the beginnings of demolition. However, that was not the end of the story. The line from Central to Garston reopened in May 1977 for the new electric service running underground from Sandhills, allowing through running from Southport and Kirkby.

The local service from Lime Street to St Helens and Wigan North Western faced possible closure in the 1960s, but it was reprieved and eventually authorised for electrification along with the Chat Moss line to Manchester, with regular electric services starting in May 2015. Today, the Liverpool-St Helens-Wigan line carries three off-peak trains an hour, compared with only two trains to St Helens and one continuing to Wigan in the early 1970s.

Of the former Lancashire & Yorkshire Railway routes from Liverpool Exchange, the electrified line to Southport and the diesel line to Wigan Wallgate via Kirkby were both earmarked for closure in the Beeching Report, which would have left Exchange station with trains on a single route to Ormskirk and Preston. The busy Southport line was reprieved, although its partly-electrified continuation from Southport to Preston closed in 1964. The Exchange-Preston line lost its through trains in 1970 and Ormskirk became a double terminus with buffer stops halfway along the station. The Exchange-Wigan line survived its closure threat, but for local traffic only. The track was physically severed at Kirkby station in 1977 in similar fashion to Ormskirk once electrification was extended from Liverpool to Kirkby, leaving a diesel service between Kirkby and Wigan. Despite the survival of all three former L&YR routes, Exchange station closed in 1977 when the underground link line opened from Sandhills to Liverpool Central.

The East Lancashire Line from Preston to Colne looked secure in the 1960s, as did its continuation from Colne to Skipton. However, the Barnoldswick branch lost its passenger service in 1965 and the Copy Pit line from Burnley to Todmorden carried only seasonal long-distance trains by the early 1970s. The decline of the Colne-Skipton line was unexpected because it was identified as a 'route for development' in 1967 and might have become the only railway route to Skipton. However, a volte-face resulted in the complete closure of Colne-Skipton in February 1970. The remaining branch to Colne was singled beyond Chaffers Siding in 1971 and all the way from Gannow Junction in 1986. Meanwhile, the Copy Pit line enjoyed a revival in 1984 with regular services between Leeds and Preston, sponsored initially by the National & Provincial Building Society. The intermediate station at Burnley Manchester Road reopened in 1986, and the relaying of the Todmorden curve in 2015 enabled the Copy Pit line to carry trains between Manchester and East Lancashire via Rochdale.

The Blackburn-Clitheroe line regained a regular local service in May 1994 after a gap of 32 years. The line had remained open in the interim for freight, excursions and diverted passenger trains. Today, Northern runs an hourly off-peak service to Clitheroe, with most trains starting back at Rochdale and running via Manchester Victoria and Bolton. Additionally, Clitheroe is served by two Sunday trains between Preston and Hellifield.

The original Beeching plans for the Fylde Coast were almost the opposite of what actually happened in the late 1960s. The intention was to close the Blackpool North branch but retain both routes to Blackpool Central – via Lytham St Annes and direct from Kirkham – as well as the Fleetwood branch. In fact, BR retained Blackpool North which became the main station for the town. Blackpool Central closed in 1964 and the track was cut

The Oldham loop had been the preserve of DMUs since the end of steam, but loco-hauled trains returned in the early 1990s as an extension of Manchester-Blackpool trains, partly in order to avoid a run-round manoeuvre at Manchester Victoria. 31467 heads south near Shaw with the 0940 Manchester Victoria-Rochdale-Oldham-Manchester Victoria-Blackpool North working on 6 July 1990. *(Paul Shannon)*

Haulage enthusiasts indulge in flailing as InterCity Mainline-liveried 37430 *Cwmbrân* approaches Burscough Bridge with the 1706 Manchester Victoria-Southport 'club train' on 4 June 1991. 37430 was officially allocated to the freight business at that time, but it covered numerous passenger workings from Manchester to Rochdale, Blackburn, Southport and Blackpool. The bridge just behind the two signals carries the Ormskirk-Preston line. *(Paul Shannon)*

back to Blackpool South; the direct line from Kirkham closed in 1967 and the remaining line via Lytham was fully singled by 1983, after which the maximum train frequency on the branch was hourly. The Fleetwood branch passenger service was cut back to the former Wyre Dock station in 1966 and withdrawn altogether in May 1970. The Blackpool North line meanwhile was re-signalled in 2017 with closure of five mechanical boxes and through electric services from Preston began in the following year.

Lancaster was served by both ex-LNWR and ex-Midland routes. Between Lancaster and Morecambe, the former Midland route closed to passengers in 1966, even though it was electrified. Trains to and from Heysham then had to reverse at Morecambe to connect with the ex-LNWR Lancaster-Morecambe branch via Bare Lane. The former Midland route from Lancaster to Wennington also lost its passenger service in 1966, leaving the Carnforth-Wennington line to carry traffic to and from the Skipton line.

Morecambe's days as a holiday resort declined and the sprawling Morecambe Promenade station closed in 1994 in favour of a modest two-platform facility slightly further away from the seafront. The Morecambe branch was reconfigured as two bidirectional single lines from Bare Lane with no connection between them at Morecambe itself; only the southernmost track gave access to the Heysham branch and included a run-round loop.

The short branch to Heysham lost its local passenger service in 1966 and then only handled a sparse schedule of boat trains connecting with Belfast sailings. These workings ceased in 1975 and Heysham then saw only occasional passenger trains until 1987, when BR introduced a daily service from Stockport to connect with a sailing to the Isle of Man. Rationalisation in 1994 saw Heysham station cut back to a single platform with a basic shelter. Today, Northern still provides a daily rail connection with the Isle of Man sailing but running only to and from Lancaster.

Gas lamps and several period cars including a Morris Minor Traveller and an Austin 1100 set the scene at Wigan Wallgate as the 1120 Manchester Victoria-Southport makes its call on 16 May 1977. The train comprises Class 105 motor vehicles M50778 and M50814 with Class 104 trailer M59142 in the middle. 40107 passes by on the then newly electrified West Coast Main Line. *(David Rapson)*

Liverpool Exchange lost its main-line status after the withdrawal of Glasgow expresses in 1970. Even the through trains to Preston ceased in 1971, leaving just the electric services to Southport and Ormskirk and diesel trains to the Wigan line. Class 108 cars M51936 and M52051 set out from Exchange with the 1157 to Bolton on 22 October 1976. Exchange station closed completely in April 1977 when the Liverpool-Kirkby section was electrified and the Bolton service was amended to start from Kirkby. *(David Rapson)*

Rainford Junction became the end of a double-track section from Wigan when the onward line to Kirkby and Fazakerley was singled in 1970. The token exchange is about to take place as Pacer 142027 leads a Class 156 unit on a morning train from Kirkby on 16 August 2016. There was once a three-way junction at this location, but it is hard to imagine that today. *(Paul Shannon)*

The Settle to Carlisle line is well known for the determined campaign that ultimately saved the route from closure in the late twentieth century. The Beeching Report had listed the line for complete closure, but initially it was the local service that succumbed, with all intermediate stations except Settle and Appleby losing their passenger service in May 1970. Settle and Appleby were served by only two daytime trains in each direction on weekdays in the 1973 timetable, one of which was the Thames-Clyde Express between London St Pancras and Glasgow Central.

While the express trains declined – the Thames-Clyde Express lost its title in 1974 and ceased altogether two years later – it was not long before the local stations stirred back into life. It all began with the West Riding branch of the Ramblers' Association chartering a special train to Dent and Garsdale on 9 June 1974. The Yorkshire Dales National Park Committee then negotiated with BR to reopen Horton, Ribblehead, Dent and Garsdale stations - although at Ribblehead the northbound platform had been removed and only southbound trains could call. In summer 1975 the Dales Rail service, as it became known, consisted of four trains between Leeds and Carlisle on Saturdays and two on Sundays. Bus connections and guided walks made the service all the more attractive.

The threat of closure fell on the Settle to Carlisle line again in the early 1980s, one reason being the need to carry out costly repairs and waterproofing on Ribblehead Viaduct. Bizarrely, Ron Cotton, the BR manager tasked with closing the line, succeeded in saving it by restructuring the fares, reopening stations and increasing the train frequency. From 1987 a local train service of five trains a day appeared in the BR timetable. In 1989 Transport

Unit 140001 was constructed at Derby using Leyland National bus components adapted for rail use. It was the forerunner of Pacer Classes 141, 142, 143 and 144. It never worked regular passenger services and ended up as a driver training vehicle until its withdrawal in 1990. The unit is pictured on one of its East Lancashire Line evaluation runs at Preston on 23 September 1981. *(Paul Shannon)*

The Preston area re-signalling scheme of the early 1970s stretched to Hebden Bridge via the Copy Pit line but excluded the last few miles of the Colne branch. Manual signal boxes remained at Burnley Central, Brierfield and Chaffers Siding. A Class 108 set recedes from Chaffers Siding on an afternoon working to Colne on 25 September 1982. The three boxes finally closed in 1986, when the remaining double-track section of the branch was singled. *(Paul Shannon)*

Kirkham was once the site of a three-way junction, with lines radiating to Blackpool North via Poulton, Blackpool South/Central direct and Blackpool South/Central via Lytham. The first and third of those routes remain open today, but the third is effectively just a long siding from Kirkham. Carrying West Yorkshire PTE red and cream livery with 'metrotrain' branding, unit 155342 takes the fast lines at Kirkham with a Trans-Pennine train from Blackpool North on 15 September 1990. Electrification has since transformed this location. *(Paul Shannon)*

Having just passed the points for the Heysham branch and Morecambe run-round loop, unit 144012 approaches platform 2 at Morecambe with a local service from Lancaster on 1 November 2016. Most trains these days use platform 1, but any trains to and from Heysham must use platform 2. *(Paul Shannon)*

In the early 1970s the only local trains to serve Hellifield were those on the Leeds-Carnforth-Morecambe route. Class 111 cars E50134 and E56091 call at Hellifield with the 1356 Leeds-Morecambe service on 15 April 1974. The station buildings and canopies evaded demolition and look much smarter today than they did half a century ago. *(David Rapson)*

Secretary Paul Channon formally refused BR's closure application, supported by rail minister Michael Portillo.

For a line that markets itself as a tourist attraction as well as a practical service, the reopened stations have been attractively renovated and the lineside has so far escaped the scourge of metal palisade fencing. The signalling has been rationalised – Dent and Ais Gill boxes closed as early as January 1981 and Horton and Settle Station boxes closed in 1984 – but traditional semaphores survive at several locations including Settle Junction, Garsdale, Kirkby Stephen and Appleby on the southern half of the line. Today's weekday service between Leeds and Carlisle consists of eight trains a day, most of which call at all stations.

BR closed the branch from Ulverston to Haverthwaite and Lakeside in 1965, but it was not long before the northern part of that line was revived as a heritage operation. The Oxenholme-Windermere branch meanwhile was retained as part of the network, albeit in much reduced form. The Windermere terminus, which once boasted four platforms and an overall roof, was reduced to one shortened platform by 1973 and the whole branch was singled to reduce costs. This meant that the through trains between Windermere and Euston could no longer operate.

The Cumbrian Coast line faced an uncertain future as a through route in the 1960s, with a proposal to close the 46-mile middle section between Barrow and Whitehaven completely. It survived, but with some economies such as the closure of Nethertown loop in 1977 and the withdrawal of most station staff. In 1973 the train service over the once threatened section comprised five trains each way on weekdays plus a number of short workings serving Millom or Sellafield. Today the service is almost hourly throughout the day, including two through trains from Carlisle to Lancaster via Barrow with a journey time of over 3½ hours.

Other local lines in Cumbria were less fortunate. The Sellafield-Moor Row branch lost its workmen's passenger service in 1965 and Carlisle-Silloth closed in 1964.

One of the most photographed passenger trains in 2004 was the Arriva service over the Settle to Carlisle line, which produced a pair of EWS Class 37s and refurbished Mark 2 rolling stock. 37408 *Loch Rannoch* and 37411 *The Scottish Railway Preservation Society* provide the power for the 1333 Carlisle-Leeds train as it crosses Arten Gill viaduct on 8 September 2004. The diagram continued with a trip from Leeds to Knaresborough and back, before repeating the trip to Carlisle the following day. *(Paul Shannon)*

After Windermere lost its run-round facility in 1972, the regular service was entirely unit-operated and any locomotive-hauled specials had to be topped and tailed. Heaton (Newcastle)-based unit 143616 heads towards Staveley crossing with the 1412 from Oxenholme to Windermere on 24 July 1990. It was normal at that time for Windermere branch stock to be supplied from Heaton. *(Paul Shannon)*

In summer 1990, BR Regional Railways operated several locomotive-hauled diagrams on the Barrow line, using mixed rakes of BR blue and Network SouthEast stock. 31426 arrives at Arnside with the 1318 from Barrow to Manchester Victoria on 24 July 1990. On that day 31426 completed two journeys from Barrow to Manchester and back, followed by one trip from Barrow to Blackpool North and one from Blackpool North to Liverpool Lime Street. *(Paul Shannon)*

A final fling for locomotive haulage on the Cumbrian Coast Line was the use of Direct Rail Services Class 37s and Class 68s with Mark 2 stock. 68017 *Hornet* and 68005 *Defiant* provide the power for the 0851 Carlisle-Barrow stopping train as it approaches Millom on 28 July 2018. All Cumbrian Coast passenger workings reverted to DMUs in December 2018. *(Paul Shannon)*

The Alston branch lasted far longer than was foreseen in the 1960s, but in the end no amount of cost saving was able to prevent its closure. The standard motive power for the line was a two-car DMU, although in the last few weeks before closure four cars were needed to carry all the 'last chance' visitors. On 22 March 1974, Class 101 cars E50225 and E56084 are pictured setting out from Alston with the 0902 to Haltwhistle. *(David Rapson)*

The Workington-Keswick-Penrith line closed between Workington and Keswick in 1966 and completely in March 1972. The Alston branch managed to hang on for a long time after coming under threat. Early efforts to save the line had included the withdrawal of station staff from three intermediate stations in the 1950s and from Lambley and Alston in 1966 and 1969 respectively. All working signalling on the branch was removed in 1966, so the line effectively became a long siding from Haltwhistle. But the line was still a heavy loss-maker and, once improvements to local roads had been carried out, it finally closed on 3 May 1976.

CHAPTER 7

YORKSHIRE AND THE NORTH EAST

As in other regions, the main focus of the Beeching cuts was the network of lightly-used local lines. Most of the rural branch lines that still carried passengers in the early 1960s now faced closure. Some local lines in urban areas were also threatened, largely in response to stiffer competition from buses and, increasingly, private cars. In recent decades, a good number of local stations have been reopened, especially in South and West Yorkshire.

The changes to local railways around Sheffield have been gradual rather than dramatic. None of the lines radiating north and east from the city were listed for complete closure in the Beeching Report, but the former Midland Main Line to Leeds via Cudworth was set to lose its meagre local service, which happened in 1968. A Sheffield-Leeds local service was restored via Moorthorpe on the former Swinton and Knottingley Joint Railway in the late 1980s, with new stations at Goldthorpe and Thurnscoe.

In the Don Valley, the two parallel routes once owned by the Midland Railway and Great Central Railway respectively were reconfigured at various times to reduce duplication and serve population centres more closely. An improved track layout at Aldwarke Junction in 1973 enabled trains on the former GCR line to Doncaster to share Midland tracks from Sheffield to Aldwarke. The opening of the Rotherham Holmes chord in 1987 enabled trains on the Midland to serve the

Until the Swinton curve reopened in 1990, trains between Sheffield and Doncaster used the former Great Central route on the east side of the River Don Navigation. Class 114 cars E53035 and E54035 pass the remnants of Kilnhurst Central station with the 1705 Doncaster-Sheffield service on 15 July 1983. Kilnhurst Central had closed in 1968, just weeks after the demise of Kilnhurst West on the parallel ex-Midland line. *(Paul Shannon)*

Passenger trains returned to the former Great Central route through Parkgate when Rotherham Central reopened in 1987, using the existing crossovers at Aldwarke and the new Rotherham Holmes chord. Pacer 142079 passes Parkgate with a Sheffield-bound local on 26 June 2018. The tram-train terminus on the left was still in the testing phase at that time. *(Paul Shannon)*

reopened ex-GCR Rotherham Central station. And the reopening of the Swinton curve in 1990 made it possible for trains on the former GCR line to Doncaster to use the Midland route as far as the newly opened station at Swinton. Independently of those changes, Meadowhall Interchange opened in 1990, while the little-used stations at Attercliffe Road and Brightside both closed in 1995. A boost for Rotherham Central was the launch of the Sheffield tram-train operation over Network Rail tracks in 2018.

The Midland Main Line south of Sheffield lost its local services in 1968, while the demise of Woodhead as a passenger route in 1970 enabled BR to close Sheffield Victoria station completely. The two local services affected by the closure of Victoria were those on the Worksop line and stopping trains from Huddersfield, which were extended from Penistone to Sheffield to maintain a service between those places. Both services used the east-facing Nunnery curve to reach Sheffield Midland, which meant that the trains to and from Penistone had to reverse at Nunnery Junction. The Penistone trains still passed through Victoria as demolition work proceeded. The reversals at Nunnery Junction continued until 1983, when BR diverted the Huddersfield-Penistone-Sheffield service via Barnsley.

Doncaster, like Sheffield, suffered relatively little during the Beeching period. Some lines had already lost their local services and the only additional station closures around Doncaster in the late 1960s were Carcroft & Adwick le Street and Barnby Dun. Recent decades have seen a revival with a new Adwick station opening in 1993 along with Bentley in 1992 and Kirk Sandall in 1991. Adwick in particular is a popular park and ride facility and is the terminus of a local service from Sheffield as well as an intermediate call on the Doncaster-Leeds route. Just over the administrative border in West Yorkshire, new stations at Fitzwilliam and Sandal & Agbrigg were served by Doncaster-Leeds trains from 1982 and 1987 respectively.

Around Huddersfield, local services on the Trans-Pennine route via Diggle were trimmed in 1968 with the closure of Longwood, Golcar and Slaithwaite stations in

Between 1970 and 1981 the overhead catenary at Penistone was used only by freight trains on the Woodhead route. DMUs ran under the wires between Penistone and Sheffield. On 18 June 1981, Class 101 cars E56218 and E51549 approach Penistone with an evening Sheffield-Huddersfield working. Huddersfield Junction box outlived the demise of the Woodhead route; it was renamed Penistone in 1989 and closed in 1998 when the line came under the control of Barnsley. *(Paul Shannon)*

1968. However, a new station at Slaithwaite opened in 1982. The lines from Huddersfield to Clayton West and Penistone were earmarked for closure in the Beeching Report, but local resistance was strong. The Clayton West branch finally closed in January 1983 after a long period of decline. The Huddersfield-Penistone-Sheffield service was under prolonged threat of closure in the 1970s, not least because South and West Yorkshire PTEs were reluctant to support it, but it survived. Its diversion via Barnsley in 1983 brought the reopening of Silkstone Common station, followed by Dodworth in 1989. Economies have been made where possible and today the 20-mile line from Huddersfield to Barnsley is single track, with passing loops at Penistone and between Stocksmoor and Shepley.

Heading north and east from Huddersfield, the local service to Halifax was withdrawn in the 1960s and Brighouse station closed in 1970 when BR withdrew the Manchester-Sowerby Bridge-Mirfield-York services. A new station at Deighton on the outskirts of Huddersfield opened in 1982, while the long-awaited reopening of Brighouse took place in 2000. Brighouse is now a calling point for local trains on the Huddersfield-Halifax and Sowerby Bridge-Mirfield routes, as well as Grand Central expresses between King's Cross and Bradford.

Railway history left Bradford with the inconvenience of two terminal stations, the ex-L&YR/GNR Exchange (later Interchange) and the ex-Midland Forster Square. The Beeching Report recommended keeping both stations open, but with their local services much reduced. On the L&YR/GNR side, the Pudsey loop line closed in 1964 and the Heckmondwike line lost its passenger service in 1965. The last two intermediate stations on the Halifax line, at Low Moor and Lightcliffe, closed in

Having survived by the skin of its teeth, the Huddersfield-Sheffield service was diverted via Barnsley in 1983 and its patronage began to recover. The extra station calls on the Barnsley route have justified the longer journey time between Penistone and Sheffield. With the former Woodhead line station building visible on the left, Pacer unit 144023 calls with a Sheffield-Huddersfield service on 28 September 2017. *(Paul Shannon)*

The services from Huddersfield to Clayton West and Sheffield switched to Paytrain operation in 1970 and the single-platform terminus at Clayton West looked increasingly forlorn. However, the branch lasted longer than others in the area, partly because of the coal traffic from two local pits. Metro-Cammell Class 101 cars E51428 and E51502 have just arrived at Clayton West with an evening train on 7 January 1981. *(Paul Shannon)*

Hebden Bridge was lucky to avoid going the way of so many local stations in the 1960s and 1970s; it kept its buildings and even some of its historic signs. The station was Grade II listed in 1978 and BR allowed an exception to corporate policy by applying a coat of Lancashire & Yorkshire Railway brown and buff. A four-car DMU led by a Derby Class 108 vehicle arrives at Hebden Bridge with the 1040 from Blackpool North to Leeds on 28 September 1985. *(Paul Shannon)*

The original station at Bradford Forster Square became too large after the gradual loss of long-distance traffic and, especially, the parcels business. Much of the complex trackwork remains in place as Class 108 cars F54195 and E53620 arrive with the 0930 Ilkley-Forster Square train on 29 September 1984. The signal boxes at Forster Square and Manningham Station Junction closed in the following month and the line was then controlled from Shipley Bradford Junction. *(Paul Shannon)*

1965. On the ex-GNR line to Leeds, New Pudsey station opened in 1967 – a year when not many stations were opened! – as a better-located replacement for nearby Stanningley, which closed in the following year. New Pudsey was intended to cater for InterCity traffic but ended up handling mainly local business for Bradford and Leeds.

The decline of both local and long-distance trains at Bradford Exchange led to the serious under-use of the ten-platform terminus with its fine overall roof. It was abandoned in 1973 and replaced by the four-platform Bradford Interchange, on a site slightly further from the city centre, which is still in use today.

Bradford Forster Square lost its St Pancras expresses in 1967 and its local service to Leeds City via Shipley – including the closure of six intermediate stations – in 1965. The 1965 cull also included Saltaire and Steeton & Silsden stations on the line to Keighley. The Ilkley branch switched to Paytrain operation in 1968 as a means of cutting costs. However, Dr Beeching's proposal to withdraw completely from the Leeds/Bradford-Ilkley/Keighley routes was thwarted by strong opposition and from 1970 their fortunes gradually improved.

The first sign of revival on the Ilkley branch was the reopening of Baildon station in 1973. The platforms had been disused for 20 years and the reopening was straightforward given that, in those days, there was less of an emphasis on safety, security and accessibility. Shipley station gained a platform on the north side of the

Ilkley station resisted modernisation and until the early 1980s it still boasted four platforms – two on the former through route to Skipton and two bays – as well as operational gas lighting. A visit on 7 August 1977 finds a nine-car Class 101 formation resting in one of the bay platforms; the vehicle numbers are E56068, E51437, E50373, E56119, E50135, E56092, E50279, E59108 and E50286. The station was reduced to two platforms in 1983 and electrified in 1994. *(Paul Shannon)*

triangle in 1979, so that Leeds-Keighley trains no longer needed to reverse at one end of the triangle in order to call at the station. Some remodelling of the Ilkley branch was carried out in 1983, including the singling of the two lines south of Guiseley and the reduction from four to two platforms at Ilkley. Station openings and reopenings included Crossflatts in 1982, Saltaire in 1984, Frizinghall in 1987, Cononley in 1988 and Steeton & Silsden in 1990. The sprawling nineteenth-century Forster Square station was replaced by a more compact three-platform terminus in 1990. Full re-signalling of the lines to Ilkley and Keighley was completed in 1994, along with electrification, and local services between Forster Square and Leeds were restored in 1995. Further station re-openings have taken place in recent times: Apperley Bridge in 2015 and Kirkstall Forge in 2016. All this is a far cry from the bleak future foreseen in 1963.

The rail network around Leeds looked different after Central station closed in 1967 and all services were concentrated on Leeds City. By that time the Leeds-Wetherby and Church Fenton-Wetherby-Harrogate lines had closed, but otherwise local services in the Leeds area had seen little change in the 1960s. The former Midland route through Woodlesford remained under threat until the 1980s, but in the end the line itself was reprieved and only the tiny halt at Altofts closed in 1990.

New and reopened stations around Leeds have included Bramley on the Bradford Interchange line in 1983, East Garforth on the Selby line in 1987, Burley Park on the Harrogate line in 1988, Outwood on the Wakefield line in 1988, and Cottingley on the Dewsbury line in 1988.

The local Wakefield-Knottingley service was a Beeching casualty in 1967 with the closure of two intermediate stations, Featherstone and Pontefract Tanshelf. However, services on that line resumed in 1992 and the two intermediate stations were reopened along with a new station at Streethouse. On the neighbouring line between Castleford and Knottingley, Glasshoughton station opened in 2005. The station at Knottingley itself was listed for closure in the Beeching Report, together with the onward line to Goole. That closure did not

After the closure of Castleford Cutsyke in 1968, Leeds-Knottingley trains were diverted via Castleford Central, where they had to reverse. The signalling at Castleford Central was altered so that trains could arrive and depart from either of the through platforms. Meanwhile the line east of Castleford – the suffix Central was dropped in 1969 – lost its regular all-year-round passenger service in 1970, when BR withdrew from the York-Sowerby Bridge-Manchester route. Class 108 cars E54207 and E53619 arrive at Castleford with the 1100 Leeds-Knottingley service on 15 July 1983. *(Paul Shannon)*

The poor relation of Westgate station on the electrified Doncaster-Leeds line, Wakefield Kirkgate suffered from decades of neglect. Some of its buildings were demolished in the early 1970s and, although the station was Grade II listed in 1979, it became increasingly run-down. In the late 1980s Kirkgate was served by Sheffield-Leeds stopping trains via Barnsley and by Wakefield Westgate-Huddersfield trains. Some of the Sheffield-Leeds trains were locomotive-hauled for a time and, on 8 August 1989, 47407 is pictured after making its Kirkgate call with the 0715 departure from Sheffield. *(Paul Shannon)*

The Knottingley-Goole line carries only a token passenger service but is busy with freight. Therefore, some terminating trains shunt into the Up loop to make way for passing freight trains before returning to the station for their next departure. Pacer 142066 has just made such a manoeuvre before setting out for Wakefield on 19 July 2007. Visible on the skyline from left to right are the towers of Drax power station, Eggborough power station and Kellingley colliery. *(Paul Shannon)*

happen, but today it is very much a line of two halves. Knottingley is a busy terminus with roughly two departures an hour in the off peak - one to Leeds via Castleford and the other to Leeds via Wakefield. The Knottingley-Goole line carries a token service of one eastbound and two westbound trains each weekday.

The largely rural area of East Yorkshire between the East Coast Main Line and the North Sea Coast lost most of its remaining local railways in the 1960s. The York-Beverley line, the Hornsea and Withernsea branches and the lines from Malton and Scarborough to Whitby all closed in 1964-65. The Hull-Scarborough line survived; it carried a lot of local traffic, but it was also busy in the summer with holiday trains. Re-signalling came late to that line, with Bridlington still boasting a full complement of semaphores until October 2021. Today the line between Hull and Bridlington carries a half-hourly off-peak service, with alternate trains continuing to Scarborough.

Harrogate would have become the terminus of a branch from Leeds if the Beeching proposals had been carried through. In fact, the through line from Harrogate to Northallerton via Ripon – which carried only long-distance trains in its later years – closed in 1967, but the Harrogate-York line defied the threat of closure and is still in use today. Two sections of that line were singled in 1972/73, but the signalling has been only partly modernised, with six signal boxes and several gate boxes still controlling semaphores today. The service between Harrogate and York has improved greatly in recent years, with a half-hourly frequency now maintained on weekdays.

Several branch lines on the east flank of the Pennines faced closure in the 1960s. The branch from Darlington to Barnard Castle and Middleton-on-Tees closed in 1964, while the Richmond branch managed to keep going until 1969 after surviving its original closure threat. The proposals to close the lines from Darlington to Bishop Auckland, Bishop Auckland to Durham and Bishop Auckland to Crook were only partly carried out – the Durham and Crook lines closed in 1964 and 1965 respectively, but the Darlington-Bishop Auckland remains alive today. The terminus at Bishop Auckland shifted from the curved former platform 3 to a new platform parallel to the freight-only Eastgate branch in the 1980s. Today's departure board at Bishop Auckland shows an hourly service to Saltburn via Darlington and Middlesbrough on weekdays.

On Teesside, the branch along the heavily industrialised south bank from Middlesbrough to Saltburn has lived through many changes, with reductions in the track layout as freight traffic declined and several stations closed or relocated as industry moved away from the railway corridor. South Bank station was relocated in 1984 to serve a new retail development. The island platform at Cargo Fleet closed in January 1990 and the Up line has now been re-laid on a straight alignment over part of its location. A little further east, Grangetown station closed in November 1991. Warrenby halt closed in 1978 when the railway was diverted to allow for the building of Redcar steel works; it was replaced by British Steel Redcar on the diverted line, but as elsewhere the industry around British Steel Redcar dried up and the station was mothballed in December 2019. Beyond Redcar, Longbeck station opened in 1985 to serve a housing estate.

Both the long rural branch from Middlesbrough to Whitby and its shorter offshoot to Guisborough were earmarked for closure in the 1960s. Guisborough lost its passenger service in 1964, while the Whitby branch, also known as the Esk Valley Line, survives today. In the 1970s the Whitby branch was double track from Middlesbrough to Nunthorpe, then single from Nunthorpe to Sleights with passing loops at Battersby, Castleton Moor and Glaisdale, and then double track from Sleights to Whitby. Various stages of rationalisation saw the closure of Castleton Moor loop in 1982, singling from Sleights to Whitby in 1984 and singling from Middlesbrough to

The Hull-Scarborough route retained some country branch line features in the early 1980s, with semaphore signalling and hand-worked crossing gates persisting at various locations. A Class 110/101 DMU comprising vehicles E52081, E59817, E52066, E54203 and E53604 calls at Filey with the 1430 from Scarborough to Hull on 29 September 1984. Filey station with its fine overall roof was Grade II listed in 1985, which prevented BR from demolishing it, but the level crossing and signalling were modernised in 2001. *(Paul Shannon)*

Having resisted attempts to close it in the 1960s, the Harrogate-York line became the domain of Class 141 Pacer units when first-generation DMUs needed replacing. 141120 calls at Starbeck with the 1309 York to Leeds service on 14 May 1994. The Class 141s were not overly successful and, despite modifications carried out in 1988/89, the entire fleet was withdrawn by 1997. *(Paul Shannon)*

Bishop Auckland station was originally triangular. In the early 1980s trains from Darlington terminated in the curved platform on the east-to-north face of the triangle, formerly used by Durham trains. Class 101 cars E51226 and E56071 are pictured setting off from Bishop Auckland on 12 October 1981. This part of the station was later abandoned in favour of a new platform on the south side of the former triangle. *(Paul Shannon)*

The island platform at Cargo Fleet lost its original buildings and gained a simple shelter in the late 1970s. As local industry declined, so did the station's footfall, and when BR published its proposal to close the station, it was found that there were no regular users at all. Class 101 cars E51246, E59572 and E50150 head east with a Darlington-Saltburn train on 20 March 1982. *(Paul Shannon)*

Beyond Redcar, the Saltburn branch is mainly rural in nature. When BR opened a new station at Longbeck in 1985, the adjacent level crossing retained its ex-LNER signal box, which by then had been modernised with a panel. Pacer unit 142038 approaches Longbeck with the 1417 Saltburn-Darlington service on 4 December 2019. *(Paul Shannon)*

Seen from the A171 Teesside-Scarborough road bridge, Class 101 cars E53265 and E54077 set out from Whitby with the 1522 to Darlington on 15 August 1983. At that time Bog Hall and Whitby signal boxes were still open, but the pick-up goods to Whitby coal depot had ceased three months earlier. The line between Sleights and Whitby was reduced to single track in September 1984. (Paul Shannon)

Nunthorpe – where a loop remains – in 1986. The line has been controlled from Nunthorpe using the No Signalman Token Remote system since 1989, when the signal boxes at Battersby and Glaisdale closed.

The first 4½ miles of the Whitby branch, as far as Nunthorpe, are more suburban than rural, and this stretch has gained two stations in the last half century – Gypsy Lane in 1976 and James Cook in 2014. Today's weekday service on the branch comprises four trains all the way to Whitby, two to Battersby, and ten short workings to Nunthorpe. The equivalent figures in 1973 were six, zero and one respectively. The stretch between Grosmont and Whitby can also carry through trains to and from the North Yorkshire Moors Railway, made easier in 2014 by alterations to the signalling at Grosmont.

On the south side of the Tyne, proposals to withdraw the sparse local service between Newcastle and Washington were uncontested and it ceased in 1963, although the line through Washington and Leamside would remain open for diversions until 1991. The Sunderland-Penshaw-Durham line lost its passenger service in 1964. The South Shields branch was de-electrified in 1963 and switched to Paytrain operation in 1969, as did the local service from Newcastle to Sunderland. Further change came with the building of the Tyne and Wear Metro. BR trains to South Shields finished in June 1981, and Metro operation was inaugurated from Newcastle to Heworth in November 1981 and from Heworth to South Shields in March 1984. The Metro was extended in 2002 to South Hylton, sharing Network Rail tracks from Heworth to Sunderland and using part of the former Penshaw branch trackbed from Sunderland to South Hylton.

The Tyne Valley Line faced an uncertain future in the 1960s with the proposed withdrawal of local services between Newcastle and Hexham. In the event, Wylam and Riding Mill stations were reprieved, but Elswick and Scotswood stations closed in 1967 and the North

Battersby ceased to be a through station in the 1950s, but it retained two platform faces as well as a run-round loop for locomotive-hauled trains. Pacer unit 143008 arrives with the 1120 Darlington-Whitby train on 15 July 1986. The signal box closed in 1989 and one of the platform lines was removed; however, two passenger trains can still cross at Battersby by using the single platform line on the 'first in last out' principle. *(Paul Shannon)*

A delightful rural scene is captured on 15 July 1986, as a special excursion train from Whitby to Billingham rolls into Glaisdale station. The stock comprises Class 114 cars E54003 and E53024 and Class 111 cars E78958 and E78708. Glaisdale box closed in 1989 but the crossing loop was retained, to be controlled remotely from Nunthorpe. *(Paul Shannon)*

Making a change from the usual diet of Metro-Cammell DMUs, 37109 passes Seaham with the 1241 football supporters' special from Sunderland to Middlesbrough on 14 November 1981. This was the second of three Sunderland-Middlesbrough specials on that date, all locomotive-hauled. 37109 was to survive in EWS ownership until 2007, when it was purchased by the East Lancashire Railway. *(Paul Shannon)*

Pelaw Junction is pictured in transition on 1 March 1982, as Class 101 cars E50229 and E56397 head west with a Sunderland-Newcastle train. The flyover carrying the Metro across the Leamside and Sunderland lines to gain access to the South Shields branch is well advanced, while a single track junction is visible just beyond the train for BR freight traffic to Jarrow and Tyne Dock. *(Paul Shannon)*

Wylam loop including North Wylam station closed in 1968. Trains were then rerouted via Dunston instead of Scotswood in 1982, enabling BR to save the expense of maintaining Scotswood Bridge. New stations were opened at Dunston in 1984 and Metro Centre in 1987. Today, the Tyne Valley Line is noted for its pockets of mechanical signalling, including overhead signal boxes at Wylam and Hexham.

On the north side of the Tyne, the Tynemouth loop was de-electrified in 1967. The 6½-mile Riverside loop via Byker and Walker lost its passenger service in 1973, while the main circular route from Newcastle to the coast and back continued to support an intensive 20-minute interval service. The line closed in 1978/79 for conversion to Metro operation and reopened in stages between August 1980 and November 1982.

The Blyth and Tyne network looks set to regain its local passenger trains after a long-running campaign. For the best part of 60 years the network has been freight-only territory, dominated by coal until the last pits and import terminals closed. Until 1964, the Blyth and Tyne network carried local train services from Manors (Newcastle) to Newbiggin and Monkseaton to Blyth. The closures left some major population centres – notably Ashington and Blyth – without a rail service and, even if the restored operation does not reach all the way to Newbiggin, it will be a welcome boost for the area.

One more local line is worthy of mention before we reach the Scottish border, and that is the three-mile branch from Alnmouth to Alnwick. It was mentioned only as a 'service for modification' in the Beeching Report, but closure notices for the branch were posted in 1966 and the last passenger shuttle from Alnmouth ran in January 1968. Some pruning of local stations on the Newcastle-Berwick main line also took place, with Belford and Beal both closing to passengers in January 1968. Pegswood and Widdrington stations were also under threat but survived.

Dating back to 1897, Wylam is one of two surviving overhead signal boxes in the North East, the other example being at Hexham. Class 101 cars E56398 and E50231 pass Wylam with the 0750 Carlisle-Newcastle service on 15 May 1982. Both Wylam and Hexham boxes are Grade II listed. *(Paul Shannon)*

Newcastle station had several east-facing bay platforms for local departures, but the need for these platforms diminished after the North Tyneside loop and the South Shields branch were converted to Metro operation. Today, a car park occupies the site of all but one of the bays. Back on 8 December 1981, Class 101 cars E50229 and E56082 rest in platform 5 after bringing a trainload of Christmas shoppers into town. *(Paul Shannon)*

The stock for the newly electrified North Berwick line in 1991 consisted of five elderly Class 305 units, redeployed from London suburban duties out of Liverpool Street and Fenchurch Street. ScotRail-liveried 305517 passes Blindwells with a morning train to North Berwick on 13 July 1992. The Class 305s were eventually replaced by Class 322 units and, more recently, Classes 380 and 385. *(Paul Shannon)*

Tracklifting on the Waverley route was complete by 1972 and sections of the trackbed began to be sold off and redeveloped. However, hopes of a revival never died. To cut a long story short, it has to be one of the greatest reopening schemes ever achieved in Britain that a 30-mile stretch of the former Waverley route, now known as the Borders Railway, carried its first public passenger trains for more than 46 years on 6 September 2015. A short section of track from Edinburgh to Newcraighall had reopened previously in 2002 as part of a park and ride scheme for Edinburgh commuters. The Borders Railway added seven stations to the network, terminating at Tweedbank just south of Galashiels. The line is single-track but includes three dynamic loops so that trains can pass each other at speed. Trains run at half-hourly intervals on weekdays and hourly on Sundays.

On the East Coast Main Line, local services between Edinburgh and Dunbar were reduced in 1964, but local stations survived at Prestonpans, Longniddry and Drem, served mainly by trains to and from the North Berwick branch. That four-mile branch was electrified in 1991 as part of the East Coast scheme. Since then, two local stations have been added to the Edinburgh end of the route, with Musselburgh reopening in 1988 and Wallyford coming into use in 1994.

In South West Scotland, the Beeching Report proposed the withdrawal of local train services on both the Carlisle-Glasgow main lines – the former

After the West Coast Main Line was electrified, the former Glasgow and South Western route via Dumfries became more of a secondary line, but it still saw locomotive-hauled trains. The delightful station at Dumfries, still sporting some blue enamel signs, is pictured on 24 August 1981, as 25322 calls with a rake of Mark 1 stock. *(Paul Shannon)*

Glasgow & South Western route via Dumfries and the ex-Caledonian route via Beattock – as well as the total closure of the lines from Dumfries and Ayr to Stranraer and the Kirkcudbright branch. In the event, the former Glasgow & South Western line from Ayr to Stranraer remained open, as did some of the smaller stations between Dumfries and Glasgow. BR later reopened a good number of stations on the Carlisle-Dumfries-Glasgow line: Auchinleck and Kilmaurs in 1984, New Cumnock in 1991, Gretna Green in 1993 and Sanquhar in 1994. Double track was restored between Gretna and Annan in 2008.

Ferry traffic kept the Ayr-Stranraer line reasonably healthy until 2011, when Stena Line moved its Northern Irish operation from Stranraer to Cairnryan, served by a bus connection from Ayr instead of by rail. The station at Stranraer is still located at the harbour, but its traffic is now almost entirely domestic. Between Girvan and Stranraer, ScotRail still runs five trains a day in each direction on weekdays, one of which forms a through service from Stranraer to Glasgow. The line is a low priority for investment and retains six manual signal boxes.

In Ayrshire, the rural Dalmellington and Darvel branches both closed in 1964 and the North Johnstone loop, which provided an alternative route between Elderslie and Dalry, closed in 1966. The Heads of Ayr branch closed in 1968 despite not being listed in the Beeching Report. The ex-Glasgow & South Western main line between Glasgow and Kilmarnock via Barrhead survived the threat of closure – the plan at one stage having been to divert main-line trains via Dalry – but was singled in the 1970s and then carried only a minimal local service south of Barrhead. A section of double track was restored between Stewarton and Lugton in 2009, enabling a regular-interval service to operate. The Dalry-Kilmarnock line fared less favourably: it lost its local passenger service in 1966 and closed completely in 1973. Another east-west route, linking Troon with Kilmarnock, lost its local trains in 1969, but remains open today for through traffic.

The line through Maybole was singled in 1973, with only the former southbound platform remaining in use. Class 107 cars 52005, 59804 and 52031 call at Maybole with the 0753 Girvan-Ayr train on 25 July 1985. Most trains from Girvan at that time worked through to Glasgow, calling at principal intermediate stations. *(Paul Shannon)*

Standing out boldly from the BR corporate blue of the 1970s, Sealink colours were applied to 14 Mark 1 coaches in the early 1980s to work boat trains to Stranraer. The operation was short-lived as Class 156 units took over the duty in 1987. Passing Dalry on 18 July 1984 is 47145 with the 1130 from Glasgow Central to Stranraer Harbour. *(Paul Shannon)*

The Largs branch hugs the coastline between Stevenston and Saltcoats before reaching the town and port of Ardrossan. Class 107 cars Sc51989, Sc59795 and Sc51987 approach Saltcoats with an evening train for Largs on 25 August 1981. Full electric working to Ardrossan and Largs began in January 1987. *(Paul Shannon)*

Gatehead station closed in 1969 when BR withdrew the local service between Kilmarnock and Ayr, but the line remained open for through trains. A hybrid DMU comprising Class 104 cars M52023 and Sc59215 and Class 107 car Sc52028 passes Gatehead with the 1000 Ayr-Kilmarnock train on 18 July 1984. The semaphore signals at Gatehead were made redundant in 1986 when the level crossing came under remote control from Paisley. *(Paul Shannon)*

The Wemyss Bay branch was singled as part of the preparatory work for electrification, which went live in September 1967. The service was worked initially by Class 311 units, similar to the Class 303s that had been introduced in the Glasgow area seven years earlier. Unit 311092 calls at Inverkip with the 1545 from Glasgow Central to Wemyss Bay on 18 July 1984. *(Paul Shannon)*

The Kilwinning-Largs branch is still busy with local traffic today, together with its short offshoot to Ardrossan Harbour which benefited from a new terminal station in 1987. Electrification reached both Ardrossan Harbour and Largs in 1986/87, although as an economy measure only one track was electrified between Ardrossan South Beach and Largs, the second track remaining diesel-only for freight from Hunterston. Today, ScotRail operates hourly services to both Ardrossan Harbour and Largs.

The tangle of suburban and longer-distance lines radiating from Glasgow Central has seen many changes since the 1960s, mainly positive. The only significant closure has been the Kilmacolm branch, which was listed for closure in the Beeching Report but actually survived until January 1983. The Paisley Canal loop closed at the same time as Kilmacolm but was reinstated as far as Paisley Canal in 1990 and electrified in 2012. The East Kilbride branch was a surprising inclusion in the Beeching Report given that it was relatively busy and served the sixth-largest population centre in Scotland; fortunately, it survived. The installation of a passing loop between Hairmyres and East Kilbride in 1990 enabled more frequent trains to run and today ScotRail maintains a half-hourly off-peak service, with one extra working in the morning and evening.

A three-mile passenger branch was created in December 2005 when Larkhall was reconnected to the network by a spur from the Hamilton loop. The line was electrified from the start, with through trains to and from Dalmuir via the Argyle Line. Larkhall has two platforms, but only one is used for most of the day. The 2½-mile Lanark branch survived a cull of Lanarkshire lines in 1964/65 and was electrified as a single-track spur from the West Coast Main Line in the early 1970s. Lanark station has two platforms but, unlike Larkhall, they are normally used alternately.

The Shotts line which originally carried local passenger trains between Glasgow Central and Edinburgh Princes Street was listed for closure in the Beeching Report. Many of its intermediate stations were lightly used and for through traffic it duplicated the higher-speed Glasgow-Falkirk-Edinburgh line. The Shotts line survived, with

Completed in 1903 for the Caledonian Railway, Wemyss Bay station is noted for its Grade A listed architecture. Unit 303073 rests at Wemyss Bay before forming the 1546 departure to Glasgow Central on 18 July 1984. At that time the station still had three platform faces available, but now there are only two. *(Paul Shannon)*

trains terminating at Edinburgh Waverley instead of Princes Street from 1965, but for many years the section between Shotts and Edinburgh carried only a two-hourly service outside peak periods. Gradually the fortunes of the line have improved; additional stations were opened at Livingston South in 1984 and Wester Hailes and Curriehill in 1987. The Shotts line became the fourth electrified route between Glasgow and Edinburgh in 2019 and now supports at least one train an hour in each direction.

The town of Bathgate returned to the passenger railway map in March 1986, some 30 years after the previous service ceased. As with a number of lines elsewhere in Britain, it was freight traffic that kept the Edinburgh-Bathgate link extant during that time, but the freight was declining rapidly and would soon stop altogether. The need for a passenger service to Bathgate was driven partly by worsening traffic congestion in Edinburgh and partly by population growth in the new town of Livingston, which would be served en route.

Initially the Bathgate branch was partly single-track and carried an hourly service. However, that was just the beginning. The potential to recreate another link between Glasgow and Edinburgh was strong and in 2007 Royal Assent was granted to restore the railway between Bathgate and Drumgelloch, which had become the terminus of the extended Airdrie branch in 1989.

The Paisley Canal line was linked to the Kilmacolm branch in operational terms and the two routes closed together in 1983. A Scottish Region totem sign is visible on the right as Class 107 cars Sc51997, Sc59784 and Sc52024 pull into Paisley Canal with a Kilmacolm train on 29 August 1981. After closure the station site was quickly redeveloped and a new location had to be found when the line reopened in 1990. *(Paul Shannon)*

The former Caledonian Railway main line into Glasgow Buchanan Street was closed between Sighthill and Buchanan Street in 1966 and trains from Cumbernauld were diverted to terminate at Springburn. With St Rollox works visible in the background, Class 107 cars 51988, 59786 and 52013 head east at Sighthill with the 0857 from Springburn to Cumbernauld on 3 April 1989. *(Paul Shannon)*

Lanark station was always a terminus, although until the cutbacks of the 1960s it used to feed services to Muirkirk and Edinburgh via Carstairs as well as Glasgow. The station was re-signalled in 1973 ahead of electrification in the following year. Units 385035 and 385041 set out from Lanark with the 1123 to Glasgow Central on 26 March 2022. (Paul Shannon)

Just over 13 miles of new double track came into use in December 2010. With electrification extended from Drumgelloch to Edinburgh, the whole line was integrated into the Glasgow area network, with through trains running between Helensburgh Central or Milngavie, Bathgate and Edinburgh.

The local rail network to the east and north of Glasgow has seen other enhancements in recent decades. The Rutherglen-Whifflet line reopened to passengers in 1993, some 29 years after it became a Beeching casualty, and was electrified in 2014. A local service resumed between Glasgow Queen Street High Level and Maryhill in 1993, using tracks that had been kept for long-distance passenger and freight trains to and from the West Highlands. The local service was extended from Maryhill to Anniesland in 2005, connecting with the North Clyde electric network.

The new town of Cumbernauld lost its direct train service to central Glasgow when Buchanan Street station closed in 1966; instead, BR provided a shuttle from Cumbernauld to Springburn, connecting with the North Clyde electric network. BR extended that shuttle from Springburn to Glasgow Queen Street High Level in 1989, initially with a reversal at Cowlairs. Two intermediate stations on the route, at Stepps and Greenfaulds, were opened in the same year.

BR completed a new east-to-south curve at Cowlairs in 1993 to make the whole operation more efficient. Another intermediate station opened at Gartcosh in 2005. Finally, electrification was extended from Cowlairs and Coatbridge to Cumbernauld in 2014 and northwards from Cumbernauld to Greenhill in 2018. Today, the departure board at Cumbernauld shows a typical off-peak service of one train an hour to Falkirk, one to Dalmuir via Motherwell and Queen Street Low Level, and two to Queen Street High Level.

Around Stirling, the network shrank rather more than originally planned. The Grangemouth branch was not listed in the Beeching Report, but its passenger service was withdrawn in 1968. Similarly, the Stirling-Alloa-Dunfermline line was a late addition to the closure list, losing its passenger service in 1968. Alloa had already suffered the withdrawal of trains to Kinross in 1964, so the town was left without any passenger service. However, Alloa was reconnected to the passenger network 40 years later, with the introduction of regular trains from Stirling in May 2008. Today, ScotRail runs two trains an hour between Glasgow Queen Street, Stirling and Alloa.

The railways of Fife also suffered more than expected. The coastal route from Leven to St Andrews was listed for the chop and closed in 1965, but the remaining branches from Thornton to Leven and Leuchars to St Andrews also closed four years later despite not being listed. Likewise the unlisted Tayport branch was cut back to East Newport in 1966 and closed completely in 1969. The direct service from Cowdenbeath to Perth via Kinross was withdrawn in 1970, again despite not being listed. More positively, passenger trains returned to the Ladybank-Perth line via Newburgh in 1975, while the Leven branch is currently being rebuilt.

The two principal lines to the West Highlands – the ex-Caledonian route from Dunblane to Oban and the ex-North British route from Dumbarton to Fort William and Mallaig – posed a problem in the 1960s. No part of that network carried more than 5,000 passengers a week, but undeniably the lines fulfilled an important social role as well as carrying some worthwhile freight. The Beeching Report recommended keeping the rail access to Oban, Fort William and Mallaig, but closing the ex-Caledonian section from Dunblane to Crianlarich so that all West Highland traffic would share the route from Dumbarton. The short Killin branch and the rather longer Ballachulish branch were also earmarked for closure. Those withdrawals all went ahead in 1965/66; however, the Beeching Report also proposed the closure of a handful of small stations on the Mallaig extension, and they were reprieved.

The last half century has seen a gradual increase in service frequency on the West Highland lines. In 1973 the winter weekday service comprised three trains to Oban, two to Fort William and three from Fort William to Mallaig. In 1986 the figures were three, three and four respectively. Today the timetable shows six trains to Oban, four to Fort William and four from Fort William to Mallaig. During the same period, costs have been contained not only by replacing most locomotive-hauled trains with units but also by simplifying the signalling. The introduction of Radio Electronic Token Block working enabled the closure of three block posts on the Mallaig extension in 1987 and thirteen signal boxes on the rest of the system in 1988.

In the 1980s Dunblane was the destination of stopping trains from both Edinburgh and Glasgow. A pair of Class 101 units is pictured in the station on 19 July 1984: cars Sc53172, Sc59049 and Sc53241 await departure from the main Up platform with the 1442 to Glasgow Queen Street, while cars Sc51458, Sc59692 and Sc51538 have just arrived from Edinburgh. Electrification reached Dunblane in 2018. (Paul Shannon)

Locomotive haulage returned to Fife Coast stopping trains in the early 1980s, with rakes of Mark 1 and early Mark 2 coaches hauled mainly by Class 27s. On Saturday 21 July 1984, 27018 calls at Kinghorn with the 1728 from Dundee to Edinburgh. Class 27s lost their remaining passenger duties in 1986 and the class became extinct on the main line in 1987. (Paul Shannon)

Oban station is pictured on 24 August 1976, with 27005 and 27044 awaiting departure for Glasgow Queen Street. At that time BR was no longer using the four-character headcode panels on locomotives, although in Scotland their use had been inconsistent in any case. Oban station was rationalised in 1982 with just two platforms remaining in use, and its 19th century train shed was replaced by a simpler structure. (Paul Shannon)

Branch line closures around Perth included Gleneagles-Crieff-Comrie in 1964 and Ballinluig-Aberfeldy in 1965, accompanied by the loss of some smaller stations on the main lines. One such station, Errol, closed as late as 1985. A more significant loss was the demise of the former Caledonian Railway main line from Stanley Junction to Kinnaber Junction, once the route of Aberdeen expresses, in 1967. It made sense to send long-distance trains via Dundee instead and forfeit the modest amount of local traffic remaining on the ex-Caledonian route.

In North East Scotland, the Peterhead and Fraserburgh branches closed in 1965 and the Ballater branch in 1966. These losses left Aberdeen with just the East Coast line from Dundee and the line to Inverness. Even those two lines were set to lose their local services. The Inverness line was particularly harshly targeted, with plans to

BR opened a new two-platform station at Fort William in 1975, located on the site of the former goods yard about half a mile further back from the original terminus. Colour light signalling was controlled from a panel in Mallaig Junction box. 27004 awaits departure time on 21 August 1976 with the morning train to Mallaig. *(Paul Shannon)*

Banavie was one of the smaller stations on the Mallaig extension that was proposed for closure in the Beeching Report, but it survived. 27033 makes its call with the 1640 Fort William-Mallaig on 28 June 1975. Banavie became the location of the Radio Electronic Token Block signalling centre for the West Highland Line in 1988. *(David Rapson)*

The most westerly station on the British mainland, Mallaig, was firmly locomotive-hauled territory until Sprinter units arrived in January 1989. It was also the last place on the British network to be served by mixed passenger and freight trains, with a few oil tanks often being added to the afternoon service from Fort William. A visit to Mallaig on 10 January 1979 finds 27032 waiting to depart. *(Paul Shannon)*

Laurencekirk has retained not only its mechanical signalling but also its station goods yard, which was used to offload pipes for the North Sea oil industry until the early 2000s. The passenger station reopened in May 2009. Unit 158703 has just called at Laurencekirk with the 1243 from Montrose to Inverurie on 30 June 2021. *(Paul Shannon)*

close all intermediate stations on the 40-mile stretch between Aberdeen and Huntly. In the event, Inverurie and Insch were reprieved, but with a service frequency that did little to encourage local travel. In 1973 BR ran just six trains a day over the whole Aberdeen-Inverness line, plus one short working from Aberdeen to Elgin and back and one morning train from Elgin to Inverness.

In recent decades more effort has been made to attract local traffic on both surviving routes into Aberdeen. Stations were reopened on the Inverness line at Dyce in 1984 and

Kintore in 2020, and on the Dundee line at Portlethen in 1985 and Laurencekirk in 2009. ScotRail now operates an hourly local service between Montrose and Inverurie, as well as an increased number of longer-distance trains.

The railways of Morayshire were hit hard in the 1960s. Passenger services were withdrawn from the following routes: Tillynaught-Banff in 1964, Elgin-Lossiemouth in 1964, Aviemore-Forres/Craigellachie in 1965, Elgin Craigellachie-Keith in 1968, and Elgin-Buckie-Keith in 1968. All that then remained was the main line from Aberdeen to Inverness, although a ten-mile stretch of the Aviemore-Craigellachie line was subsequently restored as a heritage operation.

While the Beeching Report had been lenient with the West Highlands, the same was not true for the long railway tentacles that stretched west and north from Inverness. Both Kyle of Lochalsh and Far North lines were proposed for total closure. The case for withdrawal was strong, given that neither line came close to reaching the threshold of 5,000 passengers a week. But the poor state of the road network forced a rethink and the lines were reprieved. A second attempt to close the Kyle line was made in 1971, when the government announced that the line's subsidy would end in December 1973. Again, the threat of closure was averted, this time partly because of the potential for increased freight traffic to an oil rig construction site.

In the late 1970s both Kyle of Lochalsh and Far North lines were fascinating outposts of railway operations. All passenger trains were locomotive-hauled and some conveyed more vans for mail, parcels and newspapers than passenger accommodation. The morning train from Dingwall to Kyle was a mixed passenger and freight working, and one of the Far North trains conveyed a fish van that would later be forwarded from Inverness to Aberdeen. Many stations on the Far North line retained a functional goods yard.

An attempt to revive local traffic was the reopening of Alness station in 1973, followed by Muir of Ord in 1976. Big cost savings were made when Radio Electronic Token Block signalling was inaugurated on the Kyle line in 1984 and the Far North in 1985. All signal boxes beyond Dingwall were closed at that time. However, both lines faced increasing competition from road transport. The opening of the Skye Bridge in 1995 made the Kyle of Lochalsh-Kyleakin ferry redundant and it became more attractive to travel between Inverness and Skye by road. The road journey to the Far North has become much shorter since the completion of bridges across the Moray Firth, the Cromarty Firth and the Dornoch Firth. Nevertheless, two further station re-openings have taken place, with tiny platforms provided at Beauly in 2002 and Conon Bridge in 2013. The Far North line now supports four trains each weekday over its whole length as well as several short workings over the southern part of the route.

After 20 years of domination by Class 120 DMUs, most Aberdeen-Inverness services switched to locomotive haulage in 1980. Adorned with Inverness depot's Highland stag emblem, 47482 is pictured at Keith with a morning Aberdeen-Inverness working in summer 1988. 47482 had spent most of its life on the Western and London Midland regions before moving to Inverness in 1987. *(Michael Rhodes)*

The opportunity to travel in an observation saloon returned to the Kyle of Lochalsh line in 1979 when BR began attaching vehicle 41, a rebuilt former West Coast Joint Stock restaurant car dating back to 1892, to the back of the mid-morning departure from Inverness. The venture was a success and was repeated in subsequent summers, using 41 in 1980 and 1981 and a different vehicle of Great Western origin from 1982. Vehicle 41 is pictured at Dingwall on 27 July 1979. *(Paul Shannon)*

The windswept landscape of Strath Bran is well illustrated as 26032 heads west near Achanalt with the 1745 from Inverness to Kyle of Lochalsh on 24 June 1975. Class 26s were the standard traction for both passenger and freight services on the Kyle line until Class 37s took over in the early 1980s. They in turn gave way to Sprinter units in the early 1990s. *(David Rapson)*

Mail, parcels and newspapers were important sources of revenue on the Far North and Kyle lines, justifying the continued use of hauled stock rather than DMUs. 26042 arrives at Invergordon with the first Far North train of the day from Inverness on 20 March 1981. The train will be split at Georgemas Junction into portions for Thurso and Wick. *(Paul Shannon)*

In 1980, Britain's most northerly railway station at Thurso looked much the same as it would have done 20 years earlier, with a run-round loop for locomotive-hauled passenger trains and a fully functioning goods yard. Even the former Highland Railway goods shed was still in use. 26042 waits to depart with one parcels van and three passenger coaches for Georgemas Junction on 24 September 1980. *(Paul Shannon)*

BIBLIOGRAPHY

Baker, S.K., *Rail Atlas of Great Britain and Ireland*, various editions (OPC)
Branch Line News, various issues
British Rail Motive Power Combined Volume, various editions (Ian Allan)
British Rail Track Diagrams, various volumes and dates (Quail Map Company)
Clinker, C.R., *Clinker's Register of Closed Passenger Stations and Goods Depots* (Avon-Anglia, 1988)
Rail, various issues
Railway Magazine, various issues
Rhodes, M., *The Encyclopaedia of 21st Century Signal Boxes* (Platform 5, 2019)
Thomas, D. St J. and Whitehouse P., *BR in the Eighties* (David and Charles, 1990)